OUT OF NEW
NOVA SCOTIA KITCHENS

Best-loved East Coast dishes for today

CRAIG FLINN

FORMAC PUBLISHING COMPANY LIMITED

HALIFAX

For Jacqueline

Formac Publishing Company Limited recognizes the support of the Province of Nova Scotia through Film and Creative Industries Nova Scotia. We are pleased to work in partnership with the agency to develop and promote our creative industries for the benefit of all Nova Scotians. We acknowledge the support of the Canada Council for the Arts which last year invested $157 million to bring the arts to Canadians throughout the country.

 Canada Council   Conseil des Arts
for the Arts   du Canada

Canadä

Cover design: Meghan Collins

All photography by Jen Partridge www.partridge.ca

Library and Archives Canada Cataloguing in Publication

Flinn, Craig, author
        Out of new Nova Scotia kitchens : best-loved East Coast dishes for today / Craig Flinn.

Includes index.
ISBN 978-1-4595-0392-2 (bound)

        1. Cooking--Nova Scotia. 2. Cooking, Canadian--Maritime Provinces style. 3. Local foods--Nova Scotia. 4. Local foods--Maritime Provinces. 5. Cookbooks. I. Title.

TX715.6.F565 2015   641.59716   C2015-903533-3

Formac Publishing Company Limited
5502 Atlantic Street
Halifax, Nova Scotia, Canada
B3H 1G4
www.formac.ca

Printed and bound in China.

CONTENTS

INTRODUCTION

It has been five years since I last published a cookbook, and in that time much has changed in my life as a cook. I opened two more restaurants, travelled across North America and throughout Europe and Asia and continued to promote and celebrate the incredible local food producers we have in this province and, indeed, across Canada. I am often thought of as a pioneer in the farm-to-table movement and as the "local food guy." Then, in 2012 I was honoured with the Gary MacDonald Culinary Ambassador of Nova Scotia Award, presented by my colleagues in the food industry. That experience got me seeing myself as more of a Nova Scotian chef, and thinking more about what my food represented and what I had been trying to showcase for so many years in my restaurants. I realized that what I was doing each day was not representing a food movement, creating a style of cooking or promoting something unique to me. I have always been part of a community who loved and respected, through food and hospitality, one simple thing — a place called Nova Scotia.

Our food community has recently lost a dear friend and mentor, Marie Nightingale. Her book *Out of Old Nova Scotia Kitchens* is the single most influential cookbook in my life. It shaped the way my mother cooked when I was growing up, it was a resource for many early dishes in the restaurants and it is an important historical text. Marie's book was the first to teach us about our own culinary past and celebrate the flavours of our province, and along with them, the diversity of our culture. I am proud to have known her and shared with her several long chats about cooking, and it is my deepest hope that she would be happy with this collection that aims to build on what she had started over 40 years ago: knowledge of and pride in our own culinary traditions and ideas.

You may be asking yourself, what makes this book a collection of new recipes and are these really a representation of what comes out of Nova Scotia kitchens today? We have so many influences in our cooking and we are growing and harvesting an ingredient base that continues to expand and develop. We are not limited in the same way that villages and regions were a hundred years ago, in our province or, indeed, anywhere in the world. The sense of place that we feel when we visit "old world" cultures is inspiring to cooks, even enviable at times, but it cannot be superimposed upon a culinary landscape that is barely a quarter of a millennium old. Ours is, as the wine industry likes to refer to it, a "new world." In fact, the cooking that people have come to know as every day food is very recent, perhaps only a few decades old. As we dine on pastas, paninis, burgers, sweet and sour chicken, pad thai, club sandwiches, kale salads and sushi, can we really say that we are eating the foods of Nova Scotia? Well, in my opinion, yes we can. Our food culture is diverse, and recipes have a tendency to migrate. Dishes that became culturally significant over our history became so out of necessity, defined by geography and climate, shaped by ingredients that had to be found almost daily, just outside our doorsteps. So, although my love of all things local continues, for me the recipes we are cooking today are what Nova Scotia cooking is today.

The recipes chosen for this book fall into one of three general categories. First, you will find a strong representation of older traditional recipes that may feel distinctly "Nova Scotian." These are the chowders, lobster rolls and simple country dishes that have been showcased in many Nova Scotia–themed cookbooks over the years. These are my versions of the classics, and a few have a fun twist or two that make them appeal to a contemporary palate. Many of these dishes are important to me from my childhood memories, as they may be for you too.

Second, you will find recipes that focus on a seasonal ingredient. These are often dishes that I have featured at one time or another in my restaurants. They showcase some classical cooking methods rooted in European cuisine but made simpler for home cooking.

Finally, there are the new flavours, the dishes that result from a melting pot of ideas, an endless bounty of incredible produce, an ever-travelling army of talented cooks and an age of global television and celebrity chefs. These are the dishes that a few years ago you would never think would be considered Nova Scotian but have become a part of our daily eating. Some are serious and some are just plain fun, but all are delicious.

The introduction to each recipe gives you a bit more of the back story and why I have chosen to include it in this collection. After all, as the title of the book suggests, this is what new Nova Scotia food is, to me and hopefully to you — it is not meant to be a definitive list or a lesson in history.

I have personally tested all but a few of the recipes in this book and have done so in my kitchen at home, not in a restaurant kitchen. So the recipes are meant for household tools and cooking equipment. When you first glance at a recipe, the list of ingredients may seem a bit long and intimidating. Do not fret. My recipes try to build flavour using ingredients that most people have in their cupboards, and certainly things found in any grocery store or market. I may also suggest a garnish or two in that ingredient list that you can omit if you don't have it on hand. But rest assured, these dishes range from easy to moderate in difficulty, and they include nothing that is too challenging for a home cook.

My hope for this book is that it finds a place in the kitchens of home cooks in the same way that Marie's book found a place in mine. Even if you crack the spine only once and make one recipe from these pages, share it with your own family and friends and celebrate your province, then to my mind my efforts aren't in vain, and I can return to my kitchen with a smile on my face.

Scallop, Bacon, Asparagus and Spinach Carbonara
page 28

CHEESE PICNIC: FEATURING ARTISANAL CHEESES AND MY NANNY'S
CHEESEBALL WITH BANNOCK, SPICED MIXED NUTS AND ENGLISH PUB PICKLE

RHUBARB STREUSEL MUFFINS WITH HONEY VANILLA BUTTER

BLUEBERRY RED FIFE WHEAT PANCAKES WITH GREEK YOGHURT
AND WARM MAPLE SYRUP

GRILLED BEEF STRIPLOIN WITH RAINBOW BEETS AND ARUGULA SALAD WITH
HORSERADISH GOAT CHEESE DRESSING

WILD LEEK AND MUSHROOM TARTLETS WITH CHEDDAR CRUST,
PEA SHOOTS AND ROASTED MUSHROOMS VINAIGRETTE

SPRING

SPRING VEGETABLE HODGEPODGE

PAN-ROASTED HALIBUT FILLETS WITH GRILLED ASPARAGUS, KING OYSTER
MUSHROOMS AND TIDAL BAY BEURRE BLANC

CAJUN HONEY BARBECUED CHICKEN WITH QUINOA SALAD

LOBSTER ROLLS

SCALLOP, BACON, ASPARAGUS AND SPINACH CARBONARA

STRAWBERRY RHUBARB CHEESECAKE IN A MASON JAR

MAPLE AND HASKAP BERRY SUNDAE WITH CANDIED PECAN AND
LADYFINGER CRUMBLE

CARAMEL BANANA BREAD PUDDING WITH CHOCOLATE SAUCE

MENU

CHEESE PICNIC

artisanal cheeses
. . .
my nanny's cheeseball
. . .
bannock
. . .
spiced mixed nuts
. . .
English pub pickle

CHEESE PICNIC
FEATURING ARTISANAL CHEESES
and MY NANNY'S CHEESEBALL WITH BANNOCK, SPICED MIXED NUTS AND ENGLISH PUB PICKLE

As a cook in Nova Scotia, I get especially excited when a new cheese producer opens its doors in our province. There are more and more popping up, and each one has its own distinctive taste and story. Artisanal cheeses are great served year-round, but during the most dismal parts of the cold, wet spring they are a welcome addition to our menus, especially when served with pickles and great bread, in this case, traditional native Nova Scotian bannock. The English pub pickle recipe is a twist on a

ploughman's lunch staple in the U.K. called Branston pickles. And we have all had various versions of a good, old-fashioned cheeseball, but for me, this simple recipe that my Nanny Flinn has made every Christmas is still my all-time favourite. To add to these selections, simply choose any variety of local cheeses from Nova Scotia or in your neck of the woods, starting from light creamy goat cheeses to tangy, nutty blues. Lots of variety and flavours is what works best when serving cheese.

MY NANNY'S CHEESEBALL
INGREDIENTS

½ cup (125 mL) finely chopped toasted pecans
¼ cup (60 mL) chopped parsley
2 packages (250 g) cream cheese, softened
2 cups (500 mL) grated aged Cheddar
1 tbsp (15 mL) finely chopped pimento
1 tbsp (15 mL) finely chopped green pepper
1 tbsp (15 mL) minced onion
2 tsp (10 mL) Worcestershire sauce
1 tsp (5 mL) lemon juice
1 tsp (5 mL) Tabasco sauce

METHOD

In small bowl, stir together pecans and parsley, then evenly sprinkle over rimmed baking sheet; set aside. In bowl, stir together cream cheese, Cheddar, pimento, green pepper, onion, Worcestershire sauce, lemon juice and Tabasco sauce until mixed. With hands, form cheese mixture into ball; roll in reserved pecan mixture to coat all over. Transfer to plate, cover and refrigerate for at least 2 hours before serving.

Makes 1 large or 2 small cheeseballs, feeding 10 to 12 people

BANNOCK
INGREDIENTS

3 cups (750 mL) all-purpose flour
2 tbsp (30 mL) baking powder
1 tbsp (15 mL) granulated sugar
1 tsp (5 mL) salt
½ cup (125 mL) butter or shortening
1 ¼ cups (300 mL) water
Canola oil

METHOD

In bowl, whisk together flour, baking powder, sugar and salt; with 2 knives or pastry cutter, cut in butter until mixture resembles coarse meal. Add water; mix until moist dough forms. On lightly floured surface, knead once or twice until dough comes together. With hands, form into ball; flatten to a 10-inch (25 cm) circle.

In 10-inch (25 cm) cast-iron skillet over medium heat, heat ¼ inch (5 mm) canola oil until shimmering, about 2 to 4 minutes. Carefully transfer dough circle to pan (avoid splashing oil). Cook until bottom is crunchy and browned, about 5 minutes. Turn and cook until bottom is crunchy and browned and bannock is cooked through, about 5 minutes. Transfer to paper towel to drain. Cut into 8 serving wedges.

Makes 8 appetizer servings

SPICED MIXED NUTS
INGREDIENTS

½ cup (125 mL) pure maple syrup

1 tsp (5 mL) sweet or smoked paprika

½ tsp (2 mL) cinnamon

¼ tsp (1 mL) ground cloves

¼ tsp (1 mL) ground cumin

¼ tsp (1 mL) cayenne pepper

1 cup (250 mL) unsalted cashews

1 cup (250 mL) whole walnuts

1 cup (250 mL) unsalted peanuts

1 cup (250 mL) pecan halves

Salt to taste

METHOD

In bowl, whisk together maple syrup, paprika, cinnamon, cloves, cumin and cayenne pepper. Add cashews, walnuts, peanuts and pecans, tossing to coat; evenly arrange in single layer on parchment paper-lined, rimmed baking sheet. Sprinkle with salt. Bake in 325°F (160°C) oven, stirring once halfway through, for 15 to 18 minutes. Let cool in pan on rack. Break into coarse chunks before serving.

Makes 4 cups (1 L)

ENGLISH PUB PICKLE
INGREDIENTS

5 gherkins, finely chopped

2 cloves garlic, minced

1 apple, unpeeled and grated

1 zucchini, unpeeled and grated

1 cup (250 mL) grated carrots

1 cup (250 mL) grated turnips

1 cup (250 mL) finely crumbled cauliflower florets

1 cup (250 mL) finely sliced onions

⅔ cup (150 mL) malt vinegar

½ cup (125 mL) water

½ cup (125 mL) finely chopped dates

½ cup (125 mL) packed brown sugar

2 tbsp (30 mL) Worcestershire sauce

1 tsp (5 mL) mustard seeds

1 tsp (5 mL) ground allspice

½ tsp (2 mL) salt

¼ tsp (1 mL) cayenne pepper

Zest and juice of 1 lemon

1 tbsp (15 mL) water

2 tsp (10 mL) cornstarch

METHOD

In saucepan, stir together gherkins, garlic, apple, zucchini, carrots, turnips, cauliflower, onions, vinegar, water, dates, brown sugar, Worcestershire sauce, mustard seeds, allspice, salt, cayenne pepper and lemon zest and juice; bring to a boil. Reduce heat and simmer until reduced by half, about 1 hour.

In small bowl, whisk together water and cornstarch until blended and smooth; stir into gherkin mixture. Increase heat to high and cook until thickened, about 5 minutes. Remove from heat; let cool.

Makes 4 cups (1 L)

RHUBARB
STREUSEL MUFFINS
with HONEY VANILLA BUTTER

This recipe was given to me by a close family friend, Janine Durning. What I love about it is quite simple: it is an extremely delicious recipe that uses the first cut of rhubarb in my garden. Finding different uses for rhubarb is a fun challenge, and these muffins are great for entertaining at a Sunday brunch. They are not too sweet and are made with whole wheat flour, bran and a relatively small amount of oil, yet they are moist and delicious. I have also made this recipe at other times of the year using fresh highbush Nova Scotia blueberries. The unique butter they are served with is simple to make, and most people have the staples in their pantry. That's my little addition to this great recipe.

RHUBARB STREUSEL MUFFINS
INGREDIENTS

¼ cup (60 mL) packed brown sugar

2 tbsp (30 mL) large-flake rolled oats

1 tbsp (15 mL) all-purpose flour

1 tbsp (15 mL) melted butter

2 tsp (10 mL) cinnamon

½ tsp (2 mL) ground cloves

¼ tsp (1 mL) nutmeg

1 egg, beaten

1 ½ cups (375 mL) packed brown sugar

2 cups (500 mL) fresh chopped rhubarb chopped (½-inch pieces)

1 cup (250 mL) buttermilk

½ cup (125 mL) vegetable oil

1 tsp (5 mL) vanilla extract

1 ½ cups (375 mL) all-purpose flour

½ cup (125 mL) whole wheat flour

½ cup (125 mL) wheat bran

1 tsp (5 mL) baking soda

1 tsp (5 mL) baking powder

1 tsp (5 mL) salt

METHOD

In bowl, stir together brown sugar, oats, flour, butter, cinnamon, cloves and nutmeg; set aside.

In bowl, stir together egg, brown sugar, rhubarb, buttermilk, oil and vanilla. In second bowl, whisk together flour, whole wheat flour, bran, baking soda, baking powder and salt. Stir egg mixture into flour mixture until combined. Dividing evenly, fill greased 12-cup muffin tin, sprinkle reserved brown-sugar mixture overtop. Bake in 350°F (180°C) oven until cake tester inserted in centre comes out clean, 30 to 35 minutes. Let cool in pans on racks.

Makes 12 muffins

HONEY VANILLA BUTTER
INGREDIENTS

1 vanilla bean or 1 tsp (5 mL) vanilla extract

¾ cup (175 mL) butter, softened

¼ cup (60 mL) liquid honey

METHOD

Split vanilla bean in half and scrape out seeds using the back of a paring knife; discard pods and add seeds (or extract) to butter in a mixing bowl. Beat butter and vanilla, scraping down sides, until light and fluffy. On medium speed, beat in honey, scraping down sides, and process until smooth.

Makes 1 cup (250 mL)

The finished honey vanilla butter can be put into a piping bag and piped into small butter dishes or ramekins while it is soft. Alternatively, you can turn it out onto plastic wrap or foil, then roll it into a log and keep it in the fridge until you are ready to serve the muffins. Then just slice off small rounds. You can even freeze the remainder and use it again many months down the road.

BLUEBERRY RED FIFE WHEAT PANCAKES
WITH GREEK YOGHURT
and WARM MAPLE SYRUP

In Nova Scotia, spring is the season when maple syrup's made, and once the syrup's ready, a plate of warm pancakes isn't far behind. Near Earltown, a beloved sugar shack called Sugar Moon Farm serves amazing pancakes, and this recipe is my ode to that patriotic dish. The pancakes start with Canadian Red Fife wheat and are stuffed with either fresh or frozen blueberries, then lightened with the tang of thick, local yoghurt and drizzled with syrup. Warming the maple syrup enhances the aromatics, but it isn't absolutely necessary. For a wicked-good Nova Scotia meal, serve some breakfast sausages or bacon on the side.

INGREDIENTS

1 ½ cups (375 mL) all-purpose flour
1 cup (250 mL) Red Fife wheat flour
¼ cup (60 mL) packed brown sugar
1 tbsp (15 mL) baking powder
½ tsp (2 mL) salt
½ tsp (2 mL) nutmeg
½ tsp (2 mL) cinnamon
2 eggs
2 ¼ cups (550 mL) buttermilk or whole milk
2 tsp (10 mL) vanilla extract
½ cup (125 mL) butter, melted
2 tbsp (30 mL) vegetable oil
1 ½ cups (375 mL) fresh or frozen blueberries
Vegetable oil (optional), for frying
2 cups (500 mL) plain Greek yoghurt
1 cup (250 mL) pure maple syrup, warmed

METHOD

In large bowl, whisk together all-purpose flour, Red Fife flour, brown sugar, baking powder, salt, nutmeg and cinnamon. In second bowl, beat together eggs, buttermilk and vanilla. Rapidly beat in butter and oil; immediately stir into flour mixture just until batter forms. Fold in blueberries.

Place nonstick pan over medium heat, warm 1 tsp (5 mL) oil, if desired; when pan is hot, ladle in ⅓ cup (75 mL) batter for each pancake. Cook until bubbles form in centre and bottom is golden, about 4 minutes; turn and cook until bottom is golden. Set aside and keep warm.

On individual warmed serving plates, stack 2 or 3 pancakes in centre of each; top with dollop of yoghurt, then fresh blueberries. Drizzle with maple syrup.

Makes 12 pancakes

GRILLED BEEF STRIPLOIN
WITH RAINBOW BEETS AND ARUGULA SALAD
with HORSERADISH GOAT CHEESE DRESSING

One of the most challenging times of year to eat vibrant fresh salads is in the early spring, assuming that you avoid the imported organic greens in your grocery store. This salad is an homage to the many new and thriving grass-fed beef producers in the province. It also showcases beets in a new and exciting way, and uses arugula, one of the first leafy greens we see each year, right after spinach and sorrel. This is also a great entrée salad, perfect for those who enjoy a good steak but may be trying to avoid extra carbs and are lightening up their diet. It's also a friendly reminder of the charcoal barbecue that's waiting in the backyard — time to get grilling again! You can serve this as is or with a fresh baguette for a great spring supper.

GRILLED BEEF STRIPLOIN
INGREDIENTS

2 striploin grilling steaks (about 1 lb/450 g), 1 ¹/₂-inches (5 mm) thick

1 clove garlic, thinly sliced

1 shallot, thinly sliced

1 tbsp (15 mL) Worcestershire sauce

2 tsp (10 mL) chopped fresh rosemary (about 2 sprigs)

2 lb (1 kg) mixed red, yellow and Chioggia beets

2 tbsp (30 mL) extra-virgin olive oil

2 tsp (10 mL) lemon juice

1 tsp (5 mL) fleur de sel or other flaky sea salt

1 tsp (5 mL) pepper

6 oz (170 g) arugula

8 oz (225 g) cherry tomatoes

³/₄ cup (175 mL) Horseradish Goat Cheese Dressing (recipe follows)

2 spring onions, thinly sliced

Grated Parmesan cheese (optional)

METHOD

Place steaks in resealable freezer bag. In small bowl, stir together garlic, shallot, Worcestershire sauce and rosemary; pour over steaks. Seal bag and massage steaks to coat. Let marinate for at least a couple of hours in the refrigerator.

Arrange beets on rimmed baking sheet; bake in 350°F (180°C) oven until slightly browned and fork-tender, about 45 minutes. Let cool enough to handle. Separately cut and dice beets of each colour into wedges, cubes or slices; transfer each colour into separate bowl.

Drizzle with 1 tbsp (15 mL) of the oil and sprinkle with lemon juice, salt and pepper; toss to coat. Set aside or cover and refrigerate until ready to serve.

Drain steaks and pat dry with paper towels. Sprinkle pepper all over each; drizzle with remaining oil, rubbing into meat to help seal surface and prevent sticking.

If cooking over charcoal (preferred method), position grill rack just above hot coals with no visible flame. Place steaks on rack; grill until crusty and darkened, about 3 minutes per side for medium-rare (for well done, move rack or steaks farther from coals to finish cooking). If cooking on gas grill, cook for 1 or 2 additional minutes per side. Remove steaks from heat and let stand for at least 15 minutes.

Arrange arugula leaves on serving platter; scatter with reserved beets and tomatoes. Slice steaks into ¹/₄-inch (5 mm) strips and arrange on top; drizzle with any meat juices and sprinkle with salt. Drizzle with 2 to 3 tbsp (30 to 45 mL) of the Horseradish Goat Cheese Dressing; garnish with spring onions and, if desired, sprinkle with Parmesan.

Makes 4 entrée sized servings

I always suggest using an internal-read thermometer when grilling, to ensure you get the doneness you prefer. Every barbecue is different, and temperatures vary greatly. If using a propane grill, follow the same procedure but cook for an additional minute or two on each side, as propane grills rarely get as hot as direct charcoal.

HORSERADISH GOAT CHEESE DRESSING
INGREDIENTS

½ cup (125 mL) creamy goat cheese, at room temperature
½ cup (125 mL) sour cream
½ cup (125 mL) mayonnaise
¼ cup (60 mL) horseradish
2 tbsp (30 mL) cider vinegar
2 tbsp (30 mL) liquid honey
¼ tsp (1 mL) salt
¼ tsp (1 mL) pepper
Pinch cayenne pepper
2 tbsp (30 mL) finely sliced chives
1 to 2 tbsp (15 to 30 mL) water (optional)

METHOD

In food processor, combine goat cheese, sour cream, mayonnaise, horseradish, vinegar, honey, salt, pepper and cayenne pepper; purée until blended and smooth (or whisk together in small bowl). Stir in chives; if desired, add small amount of water to adjust consistency (dressing should be thick but liquid).

Makes 500 mL (2 cups)

WILD LEEK AND MUSHROOM
TARTLETS *with* CHEDDAR CRUST,
PEA SHOOTS AND ROASTED MUSHROOMS VINAIGRETTE

This vegetarian appetizer is equally popular with non-vegetarians simply because it is delicious. Cultivated mushrooms are available year-round in Nova Scotia, so the seasonal ingredients here are the wild leeks, or ramps, that foragers bring to market for just a few weeks each year. It's an exciting time for cooks and chefs — when the wild leeks are harvested, spring has finally arrived! While the wild variety has a special flavour, you can also use regular leeks.

WILD LEEK AND MUSHROOM TARTLETS
INGREDIENTS

1 ⅓ cups (325 mL) all-purpose flour

1 tsp (5 mL) granulated sugar

1 tsp (5 mL) summer savory

1 ½ cups (375 mL) grated aged Cheddar cheese

¾ cup (175 mL) butter, softened

2 tbsp (30 mL) butter

3 cups (750 mL) coarsely chopped wild leeks

Pinch each salt and pepper

¼ cup (60 mL) white wine

1 cup (250 mL) heavy cream (35% mf)

¼ cup (60 mL) grated Parmesan cheese

Roasted Mushrooms Vinaigrette (recipe follows)

2 oz (60 g) aged Gouda cheese, sliced in curls

2 oz (60 g) fresh pea shoots

METHOD

In bowl, whisk together flour, sugar and summer savory; add Cheddar and softened butter. With fingers, knead into dough; form into ball. Cover in plastic wrap and refrigerate for at least 2 hours.

Meanwhile, in saucepan over high heat, melt butter. Add leeks, salt and pepper; sauté for 3 minutes. Stir in wine; cook until almost evaporated. Stir in cream; cook until reduced by half and sauce is rich and creamy. Fold in Parmesan. Set aside.

Cut reserved dough into 8 small 2-ounce (60 g) balls; on lightly floured surface, roll out each to 6-inch (15 cm) circle and transfer to tartlet cups. Press dough into cups; prick base with fork. Bake in 350°F (180°C) oven until crisp and golden, 12 to 15 minutes. Let cool enough to handle in pan on rack. Carefully remove shells from pan.

Evenly divide reserved leek mixture among shells; top with Roasted Mushrooms Vinaigrette. Garnish with Gouda cheese curls and 2 or 3 pea shoots.

Makes 8 tartlets

When I make these, I like to use 3-inch (8 cm) fluted tartlet pans with removable bases, and nonstick if possible. If you are using aluminium tartlet pans, give them a light spray with food release or grease and flour dust them as you would for a traditional baked pie. This Cheddar dough gets lovely and crisp and holds its shape very well as it bakes, making it ideal for this dish.

ROASTED MUSHROOMS VINAIGRETTE
INGREDIENTS

1 large portobello mushroom cap

4 oz (125 g) button mushrooms, crushed

4 oz (125 g) oyster mushrooms, shredded

4 oz (125 g) shiitake mushrooms, coarsely chopped
   (with stems removed)

¾ cup (175 mL) extra-virgin olive oil

1 tbsp (15 mL) fresh thyme

Salt and pepper

1 clove garlic, finely minced

2 tbsp (30 mL) sherry, red wine or balsamic vinegar

2 tbsp (30 mL) finely chopped chives

2 tsp (10 mL) Dijon mustard

METHOD

With inverted spoon, scrape and discard gills from undersides of
portobello mushroom cap; crumble or coarsely dice cap and transfer to
bowl. Add button mushrooms, oyster mushrooms, shiitake mushrooms,
half the oil, thyme, salt and pepper; toss to coat. Evenly arrange in
single layer on rimmed baking sheet; bake in 450°F (220°C) oven until
just beginning to colour, about 10 minutes.

   In glass measure, whisk together garlic, sherry, chives, mustard and
remaining oil; toss onto mushroom mixture to coat.

Makes 8 portions

SPRING VEGETABLE
HODGEPODGE

Vegetables do not thrive during a Nova Scotia spring. However, there are a few veggies that do present themselves, and treated right, they can be paired with any number of seafood or meat dishes. Hodgepodge is traditionally an early summer dish in Nova Scotia, if not the Maritimes, and is essentially a garden stew comprised of new potatoes, baby carrots, shelling peas, beans and onions simmered in milk, cream and butter. I have been cooking it for years. But recently, I have started doing this spring version and pairing it with the first halibut caught in Nova Scotia each year. However, it's a luxurious and delicious dish completely on its own as a vegetarian entrée.

INGREDIENTS

1 lb (450 g) Jerusalem artichokes, scrubbed, rinsed and halved
2 tbsp (30 mL) extra-virgin olive oil
1 tbsp (15 mL) fresh thyme
Pinch each salt and pepper
1 bunch new season's onions, with green tops reserved
1 bunch Hakurei turnips
¼ cup (60 mL) finely chopped garlic scapes
2 cups (500 mL) vegetable stock
2 cups (500 mL) whole milk
1 cup (250 mL) heavy cream (35% mf)
8 oz (250 g) fiddleheads, stems trimmed
1 bunch asparagus, trimmed and cut in 3-inch (8 cm) lengths
1 bunch red radishes
1 bunch beet greens, coarsely chopped
¼ tsp (1 mL) salt
¼ tsp (1 mL) pepper
Butter
Chopped chives

METHOD

In bowl, toss together artichokes, oil, thyme, salt and pepper to coat; spread on parchment paper–lined, rimmed baking sheet. Bake in 350°F (180°C) oven until softened, caramelized and golden, 30 to 40 minutes. Set aside and keep warm. Remove green ends from onion bulbs and slice ends into 1-inch (2.5 cm) lengths; set aside.

Halve any turnips larger than golf ball. In stockpot, stir together turnips, onion bulbs, garlic scapes and vegetable stock; cover, bring to a boil and cook for 5 minutes. Stir in milk and cream; bring to a simmer. Add fiddleheads and asparagus; cook for 5 minutes. Stir in radishes, beet greens and reserved green onion ends; cook just until greens have wilted.

Spoon into warmed bowls and season with salt and pepper; garnish each serving with artichokes, pat of butter and chives.

Makes 4 full-supper servings

A great way to wash any gritty greens is to place them in a large bowl and fill it with cold water, giving them a good swish with your fingers. Then let them stand for about 10 minutes to allow all the dirt to fall to the bottom of the bowl. Remove the greens using your hands and lift them out of the bowl into a second, clean bowl, being careful not to disturb the sand and grit at the bottom. If your vegetables looked particularly dirty before starting, you may wish to repeat this with a second washing.

PAN-ROASTED HALIBUT FILLETS
WITH GRILLED ASPARAGUS, KING OYSTER MUSHROOMS
AND TIDAL BAY BEURRE BLANC

If I had to choose a fish that was considered king of the waters off Nova Scotia, it would have to be halibut. They are not only massive, beautiful fish to look at, but they are loved by diners everywhere. The snow-white, sweet flesh is often expensive and therefore needs to be properly cooked. Its lean nature means it dries out quickly, so I use a gentle method of cooking with lots of butter to ensure success.

A beurre blanc is a great sauce accompaniment to halibut at any time, but with the Nova Scotia original Tidal Bay varietal wine, it's truly magical. If you can't find Tidal Bay, use any dry, acidic white wine you have available. This dish for me is about the ingredients of spring and less about any particular traditional fish recipe. I have served many versions of this for years on my menus.

PAN-ROASTED HALIBUT FILLETS
INGREDIENTS

1 tbsp (15 mL) vegetable oil
4 fresh boneless and skinless halibut fillets (about 6 oz/175 g),
 1 ¼-inch (3 cm) thick each
¼ cup (60 mL) butter
1 lb (500 g) asparagus, trimmed
4 king oyster mushrooms, sliced lengthwise
1 clove garlic, finely minced
4 sprigs fresh thyme
3 tbsp (45 mL) extra-virgin olive oil
2 tbsp (30 mL) grated Parmesan cheese
1 tbsp (15 mL) butter, melted
2 tsp (10 mL) chopped parsley
1 tsp (5 mL) lemon juice
Salt and pepper to taste
Tidal Bay Beurre Blanc (recipe follows)

METHOD

In nonstick saucepan over medium-high heat, warm oil just until starting to smoke; add halibut, white flesh–side down. Immediately reduce heat to medium; sear for 2 minutes, then add butter and let melt. Turn halibut; cook, reducing heat to low after 3 minutes and basting with butter, until fish flakes easily with fork and centre is firm, about 8 minutes.

In bowl, toss together asparagus, mushrooms, garlic, thyme and oil until coated. Grill over high heat until slightly charred, 2 to 3 minutes per side. Transfer to bowl; toss in Parmesan, melted butter, parsley, lemon juice, salt and pepper. Place halibut fillets on each of 4 serving plates; divide asparagus mixture evenly among plates. Drizzle with Tidal Bay Beurre Blanc.

Makes 4 servings

Checking for doneness in halibut is easy when you know what to look for. I like to use my fingers and simply poke the centre of each fillet. They should be firm to the touch but not rock hard and show no signs of shrinking. If you see any rounding in the middle or notice that the fish is flaking, they have had too much heat. Removing them slightly underdone is also fine, as residual heat will continue to cook the fish for about 5 minutes after they are removed from the hot pan.

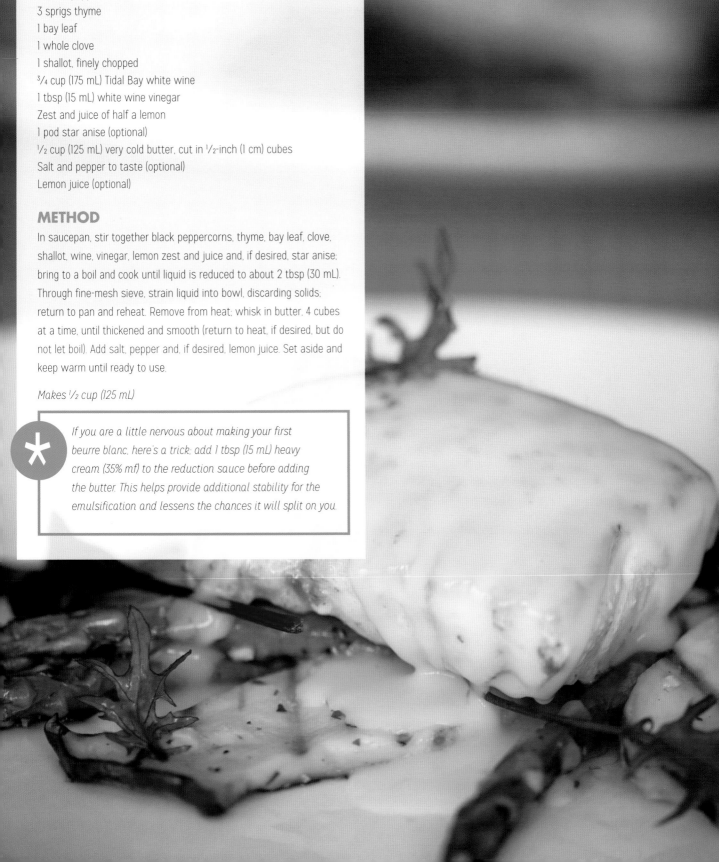

TIDAL BAY BEURRE BLANC
INGREDIENTS

6 black peppercorns, cracked

3 sprigs thyme

1 bay leaf

1 whole clove

1 shallot, finely chopped

¾ cup (175 mL) Tidal Bay white wine

1 tbsp (15 mL) white wine vinegar

Zest and juice of half a lemon

1 pod star anise (optional)

½ cup (125 mL) very cold butter, cut in ½-inch (1 cm) cubes

Salt and pepper to taste (optional)

Lemon juice (optional)

METHOD

In saucepan, stir together black peppercorns, thyme, bay leaf, clove, shallot, wine, vinegar, lemon zest and juice and, if desired, star anise; bring to a boil and cook until liquid is reduced to about 2 tbsp (30 mL). Through fine-mesh sieve, strain liquid into bowl, discarding solids; return to pan and reheat. Remove from heat; whisk in butter, 4 cubes at a time, until thickened and smooth (return to heat, if desired, but do not let boil). Add salt, pepper and, if desired, lemon juice. Set aside and keep warm until ready to use.

Makes ½ cup (125 mL)

If you are a little nervous about making your first beurre blanc, here's a trick: add 1 tbsp (15 mL) heavy cream (35% mf) to the reduction sauce before adding the butter. This helps provide additional stability for the emulsification and lessens the chances it will split on you.

CAJUN HONEY
BARBECUED CHICKEN
with QUINOA SALAD

Chicken is actually a spring ingredient for us in Nova Scotia, as the new year's flock is finally ready. I love the use of a whole bird, wasting nothing. This recipe is also a nod to the recipes of Louisiana, as "Cajun" is derived from "Acadian," referring to the French Acadians expelled from Nova Scotia in 1755. This is an important part of our heritage in Nova Scotia, and I have always been amazed at the widespread cultural influences around North America that have resulted from such a horrible period. Although one does not typically think of spicy Cajun dishes as being Nova Scotian, I certainly feel there is a connection and one that should be shared and celebrated. Should you not have a barbecue for this recipe, you can simply roast the chicken in a 400ºF (220ºC) oven for 40 to 50 minutes.

CAJUN HONEY BARBECUED CHICKEN
INGREDIENTS

2 tsp (10 mL) paprika
2 tsp (10 mL) garlic powder
1 tsp (5 mL) onion powder
1 tsp (5 mL) ground cumin
1 tsp (5 mL) granulated sugar
1 tsp (5 mL) thyme
1 tsp (5 mL) oregano
1/2 tsp (2 mL) cayenne pepper
1/2 tsp (2 mL) pepper
1/2 tsp (2 mL) hot pepper flakes
1/2 tsp (2 mL) coarse salt
1 whole chicken
1/2 cup (125 mL) liquid honey
1/4 cup (60 mL) butter
Zest and juice of 1 lemon
2 tbsp (30 mL) chopped fresh cilantro or thyme
Quinoa Salad (recipe follows)
Juice from 1/2 lemon (optional)

METHOD

In bowl, stir together paprika, garlic powder, onion powder, cumin, sugar, thyme, oregano, cayenne pepper, pepper, hot pepper flakes and salt; set aside.

On cutting board, place chicken, breast down and backbone facing you. With kitchen shears, cut along each side of backbone; remove and discard. Turn chicken over, pull open, then push down to flatten, skin side up. Cut five or six 1/4-inch (5 mm) slits into tops of leg and thigh sections. Rub reserved paprika mixture all over. (For best flavour, transfer to shallow pan, cover, refrigerate and let marinate for 12 hours.)

Transfer, skin side down, to one end of rack over hot coals with no visible flames. Push all coals under chicken. Carefully monitoring, sear until golden brown; with tongs, turn chicken and sear bone side for 5 to 6 minutes. Transfer chicken to other end of rack to cook with indirect heat. Close lid and roast, checking every few minutes and turning chicken once or twice, until cooked through, about 40 minutes.

In small saucepan, stir together honey, butter and lemon zest and juice; bring to a boil. Reduce heat and simmer for 2 minutes. Remove from heat, then stir in cilantro. Brush half the honey mixture all over chicken; close lid and grill for 10 minutes. Brush remaining glaze overtop; let stand for about 15 minutes.

Transfer chicken to large cutting board. Slice breast meat or cut chunks through breasts and ribs, then separate legs and thighs. Spoon Quinoa Salad over platter, forming well in centre; arrange chicken in well. Garnish with cilantro leaves; drizzle, if desired, with lemon juice.

Makes 4 to 6 servings

QUINOA SALAD
INGREDIENTS

1 ½ cups (375 mL) vegetable stock
¾ cup (175 mL) quinoa
½ tsp (2 mL) turmeric
Pinch salt
½ English cucumber, seeded and sliced
½ small red onion, minced
½ sweet red pepper, diced
½ sweet yellow pepper, diced
1 cup (250 mL) halved cherry or grape tomatoes
1 cup (250 mL) crumbled feta cheese
3 tbsp (45 mL) red wine vinegar
¼ cup (60 mL) extra-virgin olive oil
2 tbsp (30 mL) chopped fresh cilantro
2 tbsp (30 mL) chopped parsley
Salt and pepper to taste

METHOD

In saucepan, stir together vegetable stock, quinoa, turmeric and salt;
bring to a boil. Reduce heat and simmer until liquid has been absorbed,
about 15 minutes. Transfer to rimmed baking sheet, fluff with fork and
let cool. Transfer to bowl. Gently fold in cucumber, onion, red pepper,
yellow pepper, tomatoes, feta, vinegar, oil, cilantro, parsley, salt and
pepper. Cover and refrigerate for at least 1 hour before serving.

Makes 4 servings

LOBSTER ROLLS

Aside from chowder or fish and chips, there is no single dish that visitors seek as avidly as the lobster roll. It is such an iconic Nova Scotia treat that even McDonald's includes one on its menu. This recipe is my attempt at the perfect lobster roll. I've used some old-school garnishes, but changed it up with an interesting European-style, Marie Rose sauce. As for the rolls, sometimes you can't improve on a classic. Soft white rolls (or hot dog buns), fried in butter, are traditional.

INGREDIENTS

½ cup (125 mL) mayonnaise
2 tbsp (30 mL) chopped fresh chives
1 tsp (5 mL) Dijon mustard
1 tsp (5 mL) red wine vinegar
1 tsp (5 mL) lemon juice
1 tbsp (15 mL) ketchup
1 tsp (5 mL) Tabasco sauce
1 tsp (5 mL) Worcestershire sauce
Pinch each salt and pepper
1 lb (500 g) cooked lobster meat, coarsely chopped
2 tbsp (30 mL) minced celery
2 tbsp (30 mL) minced red onion
4 soft white sandwich rolls or hot dog buns, halved
1 tbsp (15 mL) butter, softened
1 cup (250 mL) shredded iceberg lettuce

METHOD

In bowl, whisk together mayonnaise, chives, mustard, vinegar, lemon juice, ketchup, Tabasco sauce, Worcestershire sauce, salt and pepper. Toss in lobster meat, celery and onion to mix.

Spread each cut side of roll with butter; fry in skillet just until golden. Line each roll with lettuce; evenly divide lobster salad mixture among rolls.

Makes 4 sandwiches

SCALLOP, BACON, ASPARAGUS
and SPINACH
CARBONARA

{ *Many people love the classic combination of scallops wrapped with bacon. Some may call this a dated cliché appetizer, but not me. I think it is one of the most-beloved and legitimate pairings in our ingredient base here in Nova Scotia. However, you can play with the combination and create some new dishes that speak to a more modern palate. Pasta dishes like*

carbonara are incredibly popular in Italian restaurants here, but also quite simple to make yourself. This version is one that takes the famous Digby scallop, our excellent smokehouse bacon and two of our most commonly found spring vegetables and elevates them in a very non-traditional, "Nova Scotia meets Italy" comforting dish that I love. }

INGREDIENTS

2 eggs

1 cup (250 mL) heavy cream (35% mf)

1 cup (250 mL) grated Parmesan cheese, plus extra for garnish

1/2 tsp (2 mL) salt

Pepper to taste

8 oz (250 g) spaghetti

2 tbsp (30 mL) extra-virgin olive oil

1 lb (500 g) 20/30-count sea scallops

6 slices double-smoked bacon, cut in 1/2-inch (2.5 cm) lengths

4 cloves garlic, finely minced

8 oz (250 g) asparagus, trimmed and diagonally cut in 2-inch (5 cm) lengths

1/4 cup (60 mL) white wine

2 big handfuls spinach (3 to 4 oz/90 to 125 g)

Chopped parsley or fresh chives (optional)

METHOD

In bowl, beat together eggs, cream, Parmesan, salt and pepper; set aside.

In pot of boiling salted water, cook spaghetti until firm but chewy, 6 to 8 minutes. Meanwhile, in large saucepan over high heat, warm oil; add scallops and cook, without turning, until bottoms are golden brown, about 2 minutes. Transfer to cold plate; set aside. Remove oil from pan; add bacon and cook until browned, about 3 minutes. Add garlic and asparagus; cook until asparagus is bright green and softened, about 2 minutes. Add reserved scallops and wine; cook, scraping brown bits from bottom and sides of pan, for 1 minute.

Reserving 1/4 cup (60 mL) cooking liquid, drain pasta. To saucepan, add spinach, spaghetti and reserved cooking liquid, tossing to coat. Toss in reserved egg mixture until spaghetti is coated and sauce is cooked and thickened. Garnish with Parmesan and, if desired, parsley or chives.

Makes 4 lunch servings

STRAWBERRY RHUBARB
CHEESECAKE
IN A MASON JAR

This is a dessert from my childhood. So many moms made a version of a "no bake" cheesecake, and still do, as I routinely see similar recipes topped with canned cherries or a stew of strawberries and rhubarb at church and school bake sales all over Nova Scotia. In my house growing up, this dessert was luxurious and saved for special occasions. I even requested it several times on my birthday instead of cake! The memory inspired this dessert to be served in a Mason jar. If you don't have jars, just use water glasses or even wine glasses and show off the lovely layers. Using frozen strawberries is just fine for this, as I try to use any of the previous season's fruit in frozen form before buying imported fresh fruit out of season.

STRAWBERRY RHUBARB COMPOTE
INGREDIENTS

2 ½ cups (625 mL) chopped fresh rhubarb

2 ½ cups (625 mL) fresh or frozen strawberries

1 cup (250 mL) granulated sugar

1 cinnamon stick

Zest and juice of half a lemon

1 tsp (5 mL) vanilla extract

Pinch salt

1 tbsp (15 mL) cold water

2 tsp (10 mL) cornstarch

Cream Cheese Mousse (recipe follows)

Honey Graham Crumble (recipe follows)

Strawberries (optional)

Mint leaves (optional)

METHOD

In saucepan over low heat, stir together rhubarb, strawberries, sugar, cinnamon, lemon zest and juice, and vanilla extract; bring to a simmer. Cook, stirring occasionally, until fruit releases liquid; increase heat to medium and cook until fruit has softened into sauce. Stir in salt. In small bowl, whisk together water and cornstarch until blended and smooth; stir into sauce. Cook, stirring, for 2 minutes. Remove compote from heat; let cool completely.

From eight 8-ounce (250 mL) Mason jars, remove screw bands and lids; set lids aside and replace screw bands. Smooth heaping 1 tbsp (15 mL) compote in bottom of each jar. Add layer of Cream Cheese Mousse to fill bottom two-thirds of jars; smooth tops. Divide remaining Strawberry Rhubarb Compote evenly between jars. Top with reserved whipped cream from Cream Cheese Mousse recipe; sprinkle with Honey Graham Crumble. If desired, garnish with strawberries and mint leaves.

CREAM CHEESE MOUSSE
INGREDIENTS

2 cups (500 mL) heavy cream (35% mf), whipped to stiff peaks

1 package (8 oz/250 g) cream cheese

1 cup (250 mL) granulated sugar

1 tbsp (15 mL) vanilla extract

1 tsp (5 mL) lemon or orange zest

METHOD

Set aside ⅔ cup (150 mL) of the whipped cream in refrigerator. Beat cream cheese, sugar, vanilla and zest until sugar has dissolved and mixture is light and smooth. Gently fold in remaining whipped cream, one-third at a time, just until combined. Refrigerate until ready to use.

Makes 8 servings

HONEY GRAHAM CRUMBLE
INGREDIENTS

1 ½ cups (375 mL) graham-cracker crumbs
½ cup (125 mL) large-flake rolled oats
3 tbsp (45 mL) packed brown sugar
½ tsp (2 mL) cinnamon
¼ cup (60 mL) butter, melted
3 tbsp (45 mL) liquid honey
1 tsp (5 mL) vanilla extract

METHOD

In bowl, stir together graham-cracker crumbs, oats, brown sugar
and cinnamon. In small bowl with fork, stir together butter, honey
and vanilla until blended and smooth; stir into crumb mixture until
thoroughly mixed. Press even layer into base of parchment paper–lined
baking dish: bake in 350°F (180°C) oven until firm, fragrant and lightly
toasted, about 20 minutes. Let cool completely; turn out onto rimmed
baking sheet, then break apart into irregular, pea-sized crumbs. Store
in airtight container until ready to use.

   The crumble consistency doesn't have to be perfect — texture here
is good.

MAPLE AND HASKAP
BERRY SUNDAE
with CANDIED PECAN AND LADYFINGER CRUMBLE

We have recently seen the arrival in Nova Scotia of a new fruit called Haskap berries. Deep crimson in colour, they are nutritious and tart and make fantastic preserves, amongst other things. I also love making ice cream, and it's hard to think of a more Nova Scotia-themed ice cream flavour than maple syrup. Although it is used year-round in many ways, for me, this is a must-see ingredient on a spring dessert menu. The simple Haskap berry compote below can be made and just stuck in the fridge until you are ready to serve. I think you will find this to be a bright and colourful ice cream dessert with a balance of tart and sweet that rivals the classic strawberries and vanilla ice cream sundaes of your childhood.

MAPLE AND HASKAP BERRY SUNDAE
INGREDIENTS

Maple Ice Cream (recipe follows)
Haskap Berry Compote (recipe follows)
Whipped cream (optional)
Candied Pecan and Ladyfinger Crumble (recipe follows)

METHOD

In each serving bowl, place 2 scoops Maple Ice Cream. Spoon 2 to 3 tbsp (30 to 45 mL) Haskap Berry Compote overtop. If desired, dollop with whipped cream. Generously garnish with Candied Pecan and Ladyfinger Crumble.

Makes 6 to 10 servings

MAPLE ICE CREAM
INGREDIENTS

4 cups (1 L) heavy cream (35% mf)
2 cups (500 mL) whole milk
1 tsp (5 mL) maple extract
8 egg yolks
2 eggs
2 cups (500 mL) pure Grade B or amber maple syrup
1/4 cup (60 mL) packed brown sugar

METHOD

In Dutch oven or heavy-bottomed pot, stir together cream, milk and maple extract; bring to a boil, just to scald. Immediately remove from heat; set aside.

   In heatproof bowl, whisk together egg yolks, eggs, maple syrup and brown sugar until light, blended and smooth. One ladle at a time and stirring constantly, add reserved cream mixture until blended and smooth. Set bowl over saucepan of simmering water and cook, stirring with spatula until custard is thick enough to coat back of a spoon; immediately transfer bowl into larger bowl, then fill larger bowl with ice water until just below rim of custard bowl. Stirring for about 10 minutes to speed cooling, let cool enough to handle. Cover and refrigerate until cold, about 1 hour. Transfer to electric ice cream maker and churn following manufacturer's instructions. Transfer to airtight container and freeze for at least 2 hours before serving.

HASKAP BERRY COMPOTE
INGREDIENTS

3 cups (750 mL) frozen Haskap berries
²/₃ cup (150 mL) granulated sugar
²/₃ cup (150 mL) water
1 pod star anise (optional)
2 tsp (10 mL) cornstarch
Juice of ¹/₂ lemon

METHOD

In large saucepan over medium-low heat, stir together 1 ¹/₂ cups (375 mL) of the berries, sugar, ¹/₂ cup of the water and, if desired, star anise; bring to a simmer and cook until berries are softened, about 20 minutes. In small bowl, whisk together remaining water and cornstarch; stir into berry mixture and cook until thickened. Stir remaining berries and lemon juice into berry mixture and remove from heat. Let cool; cover and refrigerate until ready to use.

After adding the second batch of berries, don't bring the mixture to a boil, but simply allow the heat of the sauce to warm through the whole berries. This gives the compote a nice, chunky texture.

CANDIED PECAN AND LADYFINGER CRUMBLE
INGREDIENTS

¹/₂ cup (125 mL) pecans
2 tbsp (30 mL) maple syrup
¹/₄ tsp (1 mL) coarse sea salt
¹/₄ tsp (1 mL) ground allspice
1 package (4 oz/125 g) ladyfinger cookies, crumbled
¹/₂ cup (125 mL) large-flake rolled oats
¹/₂ cup (125 mL) packed brown sugar
¹/₂ cup (125 mL) butter, melted
2 tsp (10 mL) cinnamon

METHOD

In bowl, stir together pecans, maple syrup, salt and allspice, tossing to coat. Evenly spread on parchment paper-lined, rimmed baking sheet; bake in 300°F (150°C) oven until toasted, stirring occasionally, about 15 minutes. Let cool, then coarsely chop; set aside.

In bowl, stir together ladyfingers, oats, brown sugar, butter and cinnamon, tossing to coat. Evenly spread on parchment paper-lined, rimmed baking sheet; bake in 350°F (180°C) oven, stirring after 10 minutes, until golden and toasted, about 20 minutes. Let cool. In bowl, toss together reserved pecan mixture and ladyfingers mixture; transfer to airtight container until ready to use.

CARAMEL
BANANA BREAD PUDDING
with CHOCOLATE SAUCE

{ *The words "bread pudding" conjure up an English country kitchen table, a printed tablecloth topped with clear plastic, a stack of chipped china bowls, a handful of mismatched spoons, a teapot covered in a hand-knit cosy and a pitcher of brown-sugar sauce — all awaiting the arrival of the hot, creamy pudding. It may sound corny, but every bread pudding I've served at my restaurants has been a dish that captures*

that homey conviviality. This version is a bit posh with its sauce garnishes and fancy presentation, but it still serves up soothing tradition. Created by my pastry chef, Yasmin Johaadien, and topped with a dollop of whipped cream or a scoop of vanilla ice cream, it's also one of the best puddings I've ever tasted. }

CARAMEL BANANA BREAD PUDDING
INGREDIENTS

1 large loaf brioche or sandwich bread, cut in ¼-inch (5 mm) slices
3 ½ cups (875 mL) finely chopped white chocolate
2 cups (500 mL) heavy cream (35% mf)
2 cups (500 mL) whole milk
2 cups (500 mL) granulated sugar
2 bananas
7 egg yolks
2 cups (500 mL) Banana Compote (recipe follows)
Chocolate Sauce (recipe follows)

METHOD

Arrange single layer of bread slices on rimmed baking sheet; toast in 400°F (200°C) oven, turning once, halfway through, just until slightly golden (do not fully toast). Set aside. In large heatproof bowl, place chocolate; set aside.

Meanwhile, in large saucepan, stir together cream, milk and 1 cup (250 mL) of the sugar; add whole bananas. Bring to a boil just to scald; immediately remove from heat, cover and let stand for at least 1 hour to let bananas steep and infuse flavour into cream mixture. Remove and discard bananas. Return pan to stove and, stirring, bring cream mixture to a boil. In bowl, whisk egg yolks just until blended; slowly pour into cream mixture, whisking constantly to prevent curdling, until blended and smooth. Gently stir into chocolate until chocolate has melted and blended.

One at a time, soak each slice of bread in cream mixture for about 2 minutes per side; transfer in single layer to greased 10-inch (25 cm)

square baking pan. Evenly spread 1 cup (250 mL) reserved caramelized banana purée from Banana Compote recipe on top. Repeat process to add second layer of soaked bread and 1 cup (250 mL) reserved caramelized banana purée. Top with final layer of soaked bread, spreading any remaining cream mixture evenly overtop. Set pudding aside for at least 1 hour or, for best result, cover and refrigerate for 12 hours before baking.

Uncover, if necessary, and set in large baking dish or roasting pan; pour enough boiling water into baking dish to come halfway up sides of pudding pan and cover with foil. Bake in 350°F (180°C) oven until cake tester inserted in centre comes out clean, 45 to 60 minutes. Transfer baking dish with pudding pan to rack; let cool for about 20 minutes. Cut into squares; transfer to individual serving plates and top each with reserved Banana Compote and Chocolate Sauce. Garnish with remaining reserved caramelized banana purée from Banana Compote recipe.

Makes 9 large or 16 small serving squares

Whisking eggs slowly into the hot cream mixture in this recipe is called "tempering," a process of slowly raising the temperature of the eggs to prevent them from coagulating into solids. It is a classic way of making custards as well as thickening a variety of sauces. Custard puddings like this are great on the second and third days, so don't be afraid to make this well in advance. When you are ready to serve, simply pop it into the microwave in individual servings and zap for 30 to 45 seconds each.

BANANA COMPOTE
INGREDIENTS

6 bananas, cut in ½-inch (5 mm) rounds
4 cups (1 L) granulated sugar
½ cup (125 mL) rum
1 cup (250 mL) cold water

METHOD

Place bananas is heatproof bowl, set aside.

Place wide saucepan over medium heat; when pan is hot, evenly sprinkle base with 1 cup (250 mL) of the sugar and cook, gently stirring occasionally to prevent burning, until amber caramel forms. Sprinkle in another layer with 1 cup (250 mL) of the sugar and cook, gently stirring occasionally, until newly added sugar has incorporated into caramel. Repeat process twice more to incorporate remaining sugar. Reduce heat to low; immediately and carefully pour in rum, stirring until blended and smooth. In small amounts, stir in water until cooking stops. Pour caramel over bananas and gently stir to coat; let stand until slightly cooled.

Transfer 2 cups (500 mL) of the caramel mixture to blender; purée. Remove 2 cups (500 mL) for bread pudding; reserve remainder for garnish.

CHOCOLATE SAUCE
INGREDIENTS

¾ cup (175 mL) finely chopped semisweet chocolate
1 cup (250 mL) heavy cream (35% mf)

METHOD

Place chocolate in small heatproof bowl; set aside. In small saucepan, bring cream to a boil just to scald; immediately pour over chocolate and let stand for 1 minute. Gently whisk in circular motion just until smooth and emulsified (do not overmix or mixture will "split"). Serve warm.

Makes 1 ¾ cups (425 mL)

> *This chocolate sauce holds for a couple of weeks in the fridge, so you can make this well in advance if you like. It sets up very hard when cold, so when you are ready to serve it, simply reheat in a saucepan on very low heat, stirring until it melts and looks shiny and silky again.*

Lobster and Sweet Pea Risotto
page 65

TRADITIONAL LOBSTER BOIL WITH NOT-SO-TRADITIONAL SIDES: SMOKED
FINGERLING POTATO SALAD, GARLIC ZUCCHINI BAKE AND GRILLED CORN
WITH BLACK PEPPER AND PARMESAN

CRISPY HADDOCK BLT

GRILLED GREEK SALAD WITH CRISPY FRIED FETA

THURSDAY NIGHT WING SALAD WITH BLUE CHEESE BUTTERMILK DRESSING

CHIP WAGON FRENCH FRIES WITH HOMEMADE KETCHUP
AND MAYONNAISE

HADDOCK, LOBSTER AND CRAB BAKE

SUMMER

GREEK LEG OF LAMB WITH HEIRLOOM TOMATO SALAD
AND FIELD CUKE TZATZIKI

FISHERMAN'S PLATTER MY WAY: NOVA SCOTIA SEAFOOD FRIED THREE WAYS
WITH SOUR CREAM AND CHIVE MASH, BRAISED PEAS WITH LEEKS AND
ROMAINE, AND BACON TARTAR SAUCE

BARBECUED MACKEREL WITH QUICK SWEET CHILI GREEN TOMATO CHOW

LOBSTER AND SWEET PEA RISOTTO

PEACH AND RASPBERRY GRUNT WITH HONEY VANILLA ICE CREAM

STRAWBERRY SHORTCAKE WITH CREAM SCONES AND
WHITE CHOCOLATE WHIPPED CREAM

MENU

TRADITIONAL LOBSTER BOIL

boiled lobster

. . .

*smoked fingerling
potato salad*

. . .

garlic zucchini bake

. . .

*grilled corn with black
pepper and Parmesan*

TRADITIONAL LOBSTER BOIL
WITH NOT-SO-TRADITIONAL SIDES
SMOKED FINGERLING POTATO SALAD, GARLIC ZUCCHINI BAKE *and* GRILLED CORN WITH BLACK PEPPER AND PARMESAN

The lobster has become an icon for Nova Scotian cuisine and an important symbol of our hospitality, so it's no wonder that visitors search out the lobster suppers they've seen in tourism promotions. It's amazing to learn that lobster was not always so prized. In earlier times, lobsters were so plentiful, they were underappreciated and considered food for the poor, but now we understand how special it is. Lobster boils are a family affair – often messy, enjoyed on a picnic table and usually served for a celebration. This gathering of side dishes dresses up a simple lobster and showcases the bounty of our summer gardens. You can serve the Garlic Zucchini Bake in individual ramekins, so guests can use it as a dip for the lobster.

BOILED LOBSTER
INGREDIENTS
4 gallons (15 L) fresh seawater
6 live lobsters (about 1 ¹/₂ lb/750 g)
Smoked Fingerling Potato Salad (recipe follows)
Garlic Zucchini Bake (recipe follows)
Grilled Corn with Black Pepper and Parmesan (recipe follows)

METHOD
In large lobster pot, bring seawater to a rapid boil. One at a time, remove elastic bands from lobster claws by grasping and crossing front claws, then slipping bands off. Immediately plunge each lobster headfirst into boiling water. Cover and cook for 14 minutes (the general rule: cook 12 minutes for the first 1 lb/500 g, then 4 minutes for each additional 1 lb/500 g).

Serve immediately, or let cool, cover and refrigerate (store with backs down to retain juice inside shells) until ready to use. Serve with Smoked Fingerling Potato Salad, Garlic Zucchini Bake and Grilled Corn with Black Pepper and Parmesan.

Makes 6 portions

If you don't have access to fresh seawater, add 2 cups (500 mL) salt to 4 gallons (15 L) water. This seems like a lot of salt, but the brininess will flavour the lobsters as they cook, so they won't require further seasoning before serving.

SMOKED FINGERLING POTATO SALAD
INGREDIENTS

3 lb (1.5 kg) fingerling potatoes

Salt

1 cup (250 mL) wood chips, for smoking

¼ cup (60 mL) extra-virgin olive oil

4 cloves garlic, minced

1 shallot, minced

2 cups (500 mL) sliced leeks

1 tbsp (15 mL) celery seeds

¼ cup (60 mL) white wine

1 cup (250 mL) mayonnaise

2 tbsp (30 mL) Dijon mustard

1 tbsp (15 mL) white wine vinegar

1 tsp (5 mL) Tabasco sauce

1 tsp (5 mL) Worcestershire sauce

½ tsp (1 mL) liquid smoke (optional)

Zest and juice of 1 lemon

¼ tsp (1 mL) salt

¼ tsp (1 mL) pepper

3 green onions, thinly sliced

1 stalk celery, finely chopped

½ sweet red pepper, finely chopped

¼ cup (60 mL) chopped parsley or fresh chives

METHOD

Halve any larger potatoes lengthwise. In large pot of cold salted water, place potatoes, salt and enough cold water to cover; bring to a boil and cook until fork-tender, 12 to 14 minutes. Transfer to colander, drain and let stand for 5 minutes to cool and steam dry. Transfer to large bowl.

Make stovetop smoker using a roasting pan with lid and a rack that extends beyond rim of roasting pan. Set pan on burner. With foil, form small tray with raised edges; evenly arrange wood chips on tray. Set tray on bottom of pan, directly above burner; set rack over pan. Arrange single layer of potatoes on rack (some overlap is fine); cover with lid. Smoke over high heat; when smoke appears around lid, begin timing process. After 5 minutes, turn off burner; let stand, covered, until all smoke subsides. Transfer potatoes to large bowl (potatoes will be yellowed slightly and have a "campfire" smell).

In saucepan over medium heat, warm oil; sauté garlic, shallot, leeks and celery seeds just until leeks are softened and translucent. Increase heat to high, add wine and cook until all liquid has evaporated. Transfer to bowl with potatoes; let cool.

Meanwhile, in small bowl, whisk together mayonnaise, mustard, vinegar, Tabasco sauce, Worcestershire sauce, liquid smoke, if desired, lemon zest and juice, salt and pepper until blended and smooth. Pour over potato mixture along with green onions, celery, red pepper and parsley; with fingers, gently toss to coat (do not break up longer potatoes). For the best result, cover and refrigerate for 12 hours before serving.

Makes 6 to 8 servings

GARLIC ZUCCHINI BAKE
INGREDIENTS

4 green and yellow zucchini, each about 1 ½ inches (4 cm) in diameter
    and 8- to 10-inches (20 to 25 cm) long, stems removed
8 to 10 mixed pattypan squash
16 cloves garlic, sliced
1 cup (250 mL) extra-virgin olive oil
½ tsp (2 mL) salt
Pepper
2 tbsp (30 mL) chopped Italian parsley
Juice of ½ lemon

METHOD

Halve zucchini lengthwise; cut into ½-inch (5 cm) slices. Transfer to large bowl. Halve smaller squash and quarter larger squash (leave very small ones whole); add to bowl along with garlic, oil, salt and pepper and toss to coat. Transfer to large shallow baking dish; bake in centre of 425°F (220°C) oven, gently tossing every 10 minutes, until vegetables are softened and golden brown, about 50 minutes. Remove from heat; sprinkle with parsley and drizzle with lemon juice.

Makes enough for 6 to 8 people

This dish has quite a bit of garlicky oil that often remains in the bottom of the casserole. Whatever you do, don't waste it! Serve it alongside the lobster in small ramekins as an alternative to melted butter. Garlic and lobster are a perfect pairing.

GRILLED CORN WITH BLACK PEPPER AND PARMESAN
INGREDIENTS

6 ears unshucked corn
½ cup (125 mL) butter
6 oz (175 g) block Parmesan cheese
Coarse sea salt or kosher salt
Pepper

METHOD

Keeping core end intact, remove outer layers of husk, then peel back remaining husk to expose cob; remove and discard cornsilk, then replace husk around cob. Transfer to large bowl; cover with cold water and let soak for 30 minutes. Transfer to grill (with charcoal grill, cook using white embers with no visible flame; with gas grill, cook using preheated medium/high setting); cook, turning every 5 minutes, until kernels are tender and husks are blackened, 25 to 35 minutes. Remove from heat. Remove and discard husks; keep warm until ready to serve.

In small saucepan or microwave, melt butter. Remove from heat and let settle until clear butterfat rises to surface; skim this clarified butter into small bowl, discarding remaining liquid.

With microplane zester, grate fine shavings of Parmesan onto rimmed baking sheet; sprinkle with pepper and salt. Brush clarified butter all over one cob; immediately roll in cheese mixture, then transfer to rimmed baking sheet. Repeat to apply Parmesan mixture to each cob, using fresh Parmesan and pepper each time. Shave more Parmesan overtop and sprinkle with pepper.

Makes 6 servings

Grilling corn in the husk may seem strange, but it's quite an effective way to get a perfectly cooked cob. The corn steams inside the husks, losing none of its flavour or nutrients to a pot of water. Then as the husk flakes off and chars slightly, some of the kernels become sweeter and golden brown. Once you remove the cobs from the grill and husk them, you can always throw them back on the grill for a minute or two to give some extra colour, as I often do, simply because I love the caramelized flavour.

CRISPY
HADDOCK
BLT

Haddock is to Nova Scotia what catfish is to New Orleans. A symbol of our table, it's also the key player in what is possibly – after chowder – the most-served dish in the province every summer: fish and chips. Another iconic local summer treat is the fishburger. Usually battered haddock doused with tartar sauce and served on a standard burger bun, it is surprisingly delicious when it's done right. My version is a cross between a fishburger and a traditional BLT that creates a better version of both. I pan-fry the haddock so it's easy to make at home. I also include my recipe for bright, lemony tarragon mayonnaise, but you could use a good tartar sauce instead.

INGREDIENTS

2 eggs

¼ cup (60 mL) all-purpose flour

½ cup (125 mL) panko bread crumbs

½ cup (125 mL) grated Parmesan cheese

2 tbsp (30 mL) chopped parsley

Four 2 ½ oz (85 g) fresh haddock fillets

Salt and pepper to taste

2 tbsp (30 mL) extra-virgin olive oil

2 tbsp (30 mL) butter

8 slices bacon

2 ripe tomatoes

3 or 4 leaves iceberg lettuce

⅓ cup (75 mL) mayonnaise

1 tbsp (15 mL) chopped fresh tarragon (optional)

1 tsp (5 mL) lemon juice

4 large slices sourdough bread (each ¾-inch/2 cm thick)

2 tbsp (30 mL) butter, softened

METHOD

Pour eggs into wide shallow dish. Sprinkle flour into second wide shallow dish. In third wide shallow bowl, stir together bread crumbs, Parmesan and parsley. Pat haddock dry with paper towel; sprinkle with salt and pepper all over. Dredge haddock in flour to coat, shaking off excess; dip into eggs then roll in bread-crumb mixture to coat, patting mixture into haddock.

In nonstick pan over medium-high heat, warm oil and butter; cook haddock, turning once halfway through, until crisp and golden, about 3 minutes per side.

Arrange single layer of bacon on parchment paper–lined, rimmed baking sheet; cover with second layer of parchment paper, then place second baking sheet on top, pressing bacon flat. Bake in 350°F (180°C) oven until crisp and browned, about 15 minutes; transfer to paper towel to drain.

Discarding tough stem ends, slice tomatoes ¼-inch (5 mm) thick; sprinkle with salt and pepper.

Chiffonade lettuce by rolling up 3 or 4 leaves together, then slicing into ¼-inch (5 mm) strips; transfer to bowl, cover and refrigerate until ready to use.

In small bowl, stir together mayonnaise, tarragon, if using, and lemon juice; cover and refrigerate until ready to use.

Toast bread slices, butter both sides of each, then spread with reserved mayonnaise mixture. Place 2 haddock fillets on 2 slices of bread; top with 4 slices bacon, 3 slices tomato and half the lettuce. Top with other 2 slices; with serrated knife, gently cut each sandwich in half.

Makes 2 hearty sandwiches

GRILLED
GREEK SALAD
with CRISPY FRIED FETA

Aylesford, Nova Scotia, boasts Nick and Susan Tziolas, two fabulous cheesemakers. Nick was born and raised in Greece and moved to Nova Scotia in 1985 to begin making authentic feta cheese. Their Holmestead feta is absolutely the best on the market — and this recipe is my thanks to them and the wonderful Greek dishes that liven up my summers. A Nova Scotia menu staple, Greek salad is often served with iceberg or romaine lettuce. In my opinion, either of these choices dilutes the flavour and detracts from the colourful vegetables in the mix. In my updated version, some of the vegetables are grilled. I've also panko-crusted and fried the cheese — the warm feta is creamy and perfectly brined, just the right seasoning for the vegetables. Imported feta can be dry and over-brined, so I recommend that you search out a locally made feta.

GREEK SALAD
INGREDIENTS

1 sweet red pepper

1 sweet yellow pepper

1 sweet green pepper

1 large red onion

1 green zucchini

1 yellow zucchini

Olive oil

¼ cup (60 mL) all-purpose flour

2 eggs, beaten

½ cup (125 mL) panko bread crumbs

10 oz (300 g) block feta cheese

2 cups (500 mL) canola or vegetable oil, for frying

2 to 3 ripe tomatoes, sliced

1 English cucumber, sliced

1 cup (250 mL) kalamata olives

1 cup (250 mL) mixed baby lettuce, such as mizuna, mâche or arugula (optional)

Dressing (recipe follows)

METHOD

On grill set to high, cover and char red, yellow and green peppers, turning occasionally, until skin has darkened and blistered, 8 to 10 minutes; transfer to bowl and cover with plastic wrap. Let cool enough to handle. Remove and discard skins, seeds and cores; slice lengthwise into ¼-inch (5 mm) strips. Set aside.

Slice onion widthwise into ¼-inch (5 mm) rings. Slice zucchini lengthwise into ⅛-inch (3 mm) strips. Brush onion and zucchini all over with oil; grill, turning occasionally, until charred, about 5 minutes per side for onion and 2 to 3 minutes per side for zucchini. Set aside.

In shallow dish, sprinkle flour. In second shallow dish, stir together eggs and bread crumbs. Cut feta into 7 or 8 triangles or rectangles about ½-inch (1 cm) thick; dredge each in flour, then dip into egg mixture, turning to coat. In large steep-sided pot, heat oil until thermometer registers 350°F (180°C); carefully transfer feta to oil and cook until crisp and browned, about 2 minutes.

Arrange tomatoes and cucumber on serving platter; arrange reserved peppers, onion and zucchini overtop. Garnish with olives and, if desired, lettuce. Drizzle with Dressing. Top with feta.

Makes 6 to 8 servings

DRESSING
INGREDIENTS

2 cloves garlic, minced

¼ cup (60 mL) extra-virgin olive oil

1 tbsp (15 mL) red wine or sherry vinegar

2 tsp (10 mL) Dijon mustard

2 tsp (10 mL) liquid honey

1 tsp (5 mL) oregano

Zest and juice of 1 lemon

Salt and pepper to taste

METHOD

In bowl, whisk together garlic, oil, wine, mustard, honey, oregano, lemon zest and juice, and salt and pepper.

THURSDAY NIGHT WING SALAD

with BLUE CHEESE BUTTERMILK DRESSING

The tradition of going out for wings on Thursday nights in Nova Scotia is so popular that there are competitions and prizes awarded to those fine establishments that out-fry and out-season these delicacies each year. In this recipe, I barbecue the wings, however, both to reduce the calories but also because most people would not tend to try deep-frying this volume of chicken at home. I also like to make it a meal with some class by turning it into a salad. For me, crisp iceberg lettuce is a perfect vehicle here for the creamy blue cheese dressing, highlighting another artisanal cheese Nova Scotia is famous for.

WING SALAD
INGREDIENTS

3 lb (1.5 kg) large chicken wings
½ cup (125 mL) hot sauce, such as Frank's RedHot or Famous Dave's
1 tbsp (15 mL) water
1 tsp (5 mL) lemon juice
½ tsp (2 mL) garlic powder
½ tsp (2 mL) salt
½ tsp (2 mL) pepper
¼ tsp (1 mL) cayenne pepper
½ cup (125 mL) cold butter, cubed
1 head iceberg lettuce
1 head celery
6 to 7 baby carrots
2 ripe field tomatoes, cut in wedges
1 cup (250 mL) Blue Cheese Buttermilk Dressing (recipe follows)
Chopped fresh chives (optional)

METHOD

Preheat barbecue grill to medium-low, ensuring rack is clean, and leaving one burner off to provide a cool zone where you can move wings and prevent scorching if there are flare-ups. Arrange wings in single layer over heat; cook, uncovered and turning often, until cooked through and lightly browned all over, 30 to 40 minutes (if skin is scorching, move wings to cool side, cover with lid and cook until cooked through).

In saucepan, stir together hot sauce, water and lemon juice; bring to a gentle simmer. Stir in garlic powder, salt, pepper and cayenne pepper. Remove the pan from the heat and whisk in butter until emulsified and smooth. Set sauce aside until ready to serve.

Remove and discard core from lettuce; coarsely tear leaves. Transfer to large bowl filled with lukewarm water and let soak for 30 minutes. Fill second large bowl with ice water; plunge in lettuce and let soak for 10 minutes. Transfer to salad spinner and drain. Set aside. Remove and discard tough outer stalks and leaves from celery; separate remaining stalks, rinse and slice as desired, saving some tender leaves for garnish. Set aside. With mandoline, knife or box grater, cut carrots into fine lengthwise slices. Set aside.

Evenly divide lettuce among 4 large individual serving bowls; top with carrots, celery and tomatoes. In large bowl, toss reserved wings with the buttery hot sauce until well coated. With tongs, transfer 6 or 7 wings to centre of each salad; garnish with reserved celery leaves. Drizzle with Blue Cheese Buttermilk Dressing and, if desired, chives.

Makes 4 generous servings

The key to grilling wings is to turn them often and use medium-low heat. So, once you begin, don't go far from the grill, and don't lower the lid of the barbecue or the intense heat will render out the fat from the skin too quickly and an inferno will result.

You can make the sauce as mild or as crazy-hot as you would like by adjusting the cayenne pepper, or by adding an additional hot sauce like Sriracha or Tabasco sauce.

BLUE CHEESE BUTTERMILK DRESSING
INGREDIENTS
2 cloves garlic, minced
1/2 shallot, minced
1/2 cup (125 mL) organic sour cream
1/2 cup (125 mL) buttermilk
1/3 cup (75 mL) crumbled blue cheese
1/4 cup (60 mL) cider vinegar
1/4 cup (60 mL) liquid honey
1 tsp (5 mL) Tabasco sauce or hot sauce
1 tsp (5 mL) Dijon mustard
1/2 tsp (2 mL) salt
1/2 tsp (2 mL) pepper
1/2 cup (125 mL) canola oil
2 tbsp (30 mL) chopped fresh chives

METHOD

In blender, purée garlic, shallot, sour cream, buttermilk, blue cheese, vinegar, honey, Tabasco sauce, mustard, salt and pepper until blended and smooth. Transfer to airtight container; whisking constantly, add oil in slow, steady stream until thickened and smooth. Stir in chives. Cover and refrigerate for up to 2 weeks until ready to use.

Makes 2 cups (500 mL)

CHIP WAGON FRENCH FRIES

WITH HOMEMADE KETCHUP
and MAYONNAISE

More and more food trucks are serving upscale, indulgence foods, but the chip wagons have always been around. Everyone knows the smell of a Nova Scotia sidewalk in summer when we walk by a white van with steam billowing from its stacks. A global street food, the humble fries are also a staple in this province. Proper preparation is important and well worth the effort. Here in Nova Scotia, the Russet Burbank potato is traditionally used for fries, but I really prefer the yellow-fleshed Yukon Gold, perhaps

because I've tasted various golden chips in the U.K., France, the Netherlands and Belgium, where Bintje or Maris Piper spuds are often served. These fry to a beautiful colour outside and keep their lovely creamy interior, but you can use what you have. I've also suggested a European-style homemade mayonnaise as well as a homemade ketchup for dipping. Although mayonnaise may be less common here, it's a favourite in Belgium and Holland for a reason — it's incredibly good!

FRENCH FRIES
INGREDIENTS

2 lb (1 kg) large Russet Burbank or other russet potatoes
8 cups (2 L) peanut or vegetable oil
1 tbsp (15 mL) flaky sea salt, such as fleur de sel
Ketchup (recipe follows)
Mayonnaise (recipe follows)

METHOD

Peel sides of potatoes, leaving ends unpeeled; slice lengthwise into 1/4-inch (5 mm) batons and transfer into bowl of cold water. Let soak for at least 30 minutes.

In deep, straight-sided stockpot, heat oil until thermometer registers 300°F (150°C). Drain potatoes and pat dry with paper towels. Carefully add to oil; cook until opaque and softened but not falling apart, 5 to 6 minutes. Using slotted spoon, carefully transfer to paper towel to drain (if desired, store at room temperature for up to 2 hours until ready to use).

Heat oil again until thermometer registers 350°F (180°C). Carefully add reserved potatoes; cook until crisp and golden, 5 to 6 minutes. Using slotted spoon, carefully transfer to large bowl; immediately sprinkle with salt and toss to coat. Serve with Ketchup and Mayonnaise.

KETCHUP
INGREDIENTS

2 tbsp (30 mL) vegetable oil
4 cloves garlic, minced
1 onion, minced
1 large can (28 oz/796 mL) crushed tomatoes
1 cup (250 mL) tomato paste
1/2 cup (125 mL) corn syrup
1/2 cup (125 mL) red wine vinegar
1/4 cup (60 mL) packed brown sugar
1 tsp (5 mL) dry mustard
1/2 tsp (2 mL) ground cloves
1/2 tsp (2 mL) ground allspice
1/2 tsp (2 mL) salt
Pinch cayenne pepper

METHOD

In saucepan over high heat, warm oil; sauté garlic and onion until softened and beginning to colour. Stir in tomatoes, tomato paste, corn syrup, vinegar, brown sugar, mustard, cloves, allspice, salt and cayenne pepper; reduce heat and simmer uncovered for 30 minutes until sauce is reduced by 25 percent. Remove from heat. With immersion blender, purée until smooth and blended. Transfer to airtight container and refrigerate for up to 2 weeks or until ready to use.

Makes 2 1/2 cups (625 mL)

MAYONNAISE
INGREDIENTS

2 egg yolks

1 tbsp (15 mL) white wine vinegar

2 tsp (10 mL) Dijon mustard

2 cups (500 mL) canola, vegetable or light olive oil (or a combination of 2 or more)

Juice of ½ lemon

1 tsp (5 mL) salt

Pinch cayenne pepper

METHOD

In round-bottomed bowl, whisk together egg yolks, vinegar and mustard until blended and smooth. From glass measure and whisking constantly, add a few drops oil at a time until mixture emulsifies and thickens, then pour in remaining oil in slow, steady stream, whisking constantly, until fully emulsified. Stir in lemon juice, salt and cayenne pepper. Transfer to airtight container and refrigerate for up to 5 days or until ready to use.

Makes 2 cups (500 mL)

When whisking a mayonnaise by hand, you can secure the bowl on the counter with a tea towel wrapped around the base, as the bowl will slip and slide if unsecured. You can also make this in a food processor, but I love the control I have over the consistency by using a whisk. If your emulsification does separate, don't panic! Simply add a teaspoon of cold water and start whisking again – it should come back together right away.

HADDOCK, LOBSTER
and CRAB BAKE

Ridiculously easy to prepare, this casserole brims with luxurious ingredients, so it suits any special occasion. Crusty, baked fish-and-seafood dishes are a longstanding Nova Scotia tradition, but this upscale recipe reflects the influence of the French chefs who were imported here in the latter part

of the twentieth century at the bequest of hoteliers and finer tourist restaurants. Like all great cooks, they enthusiastically embraced local ingredients. My version celebrates three varieties of seafood in a classic velouté, a staple in every French chef's seafood-sauce repertoire.

INGREDIENTS

3 lb (1.5 kg) haddock fillets (about 3 large)
1/4 cup (60 mL) butter
1/2 cup (125 mL) finely chopped shallots
1/4 cup (60 mL) all-purpose flour
1 cup (250 mL) white wine
1 cup (250 mL) fish stock or bouillon
2/3 cup (175 mL) cream cheese
1/2 cup (125 mL) heavy cream (35% mf)
1/4 tsp (1 mL) salt
1/4 tsp (1 mL) white pepper
Scant pinch cayenne pepper
6 oz (175 g) cooked snow crab meat
12 oz (375 g) cooked lobster meat, cut in small chunks
1 tbsp (15 mL) chopped fresh tarragon
1 tbsp (15 mL) chopped fresh chives
2 tbsp (30 mL) butter
3/4 cup (175 mL) panko or fresh bread crumbs
1 tbsp (15 mL) chopped parsley

METHOD

In buttered ceramic baking dish sprinkled with salt and pepper, arrange haddock, skin side down, tucking last 2 inches (5 cm) of each tail under fillet to prevent overcooking of thinner ends. Set aside.

In saucepan over medium heat, melt 1/4 cup (60 mL) butter; gently sauté shallots just until translucent (do not brown). Sprinkle in flour; cook, stirring, for 2 minutes. Add wine and cook, whisking constantly, until smooth and thickened, about 3 minutes. Stir in fish stock, cream cheese, cream, salt, white pepper and cayenne pepper. Reduce heat to low; cook, stirring, until cream cheese is melted and mixture has thickened and warmed through, about 5 minutes. Remove from heat; gently fold in crab meat, lobster, tarragon and chives. Pour evenly over haddock.

In skillet over medium-high heat, melt 2 tbsp (30 mL) butter; stir in bread crumbs and parsley and toast just until beginning to brown. Evenly sprinkle over haddock. Bake in centre of 350°F (180°C) oven until fish is opaque, flakes easily with fork and is firm in centre, 20 to 25 minutes.

Makes 6 entrée servings

*

Panko bread crumbs were once unknown but are now a very common staple in people's pantries. However, if you have either fresh or stale bread kicking around, you can make your own bread crumbs by either pulsing the slices in a food processor or even by using the coarse side of a box grater. The texture may be more rustic, but the crumbs will still be golden brown and delicious when the dish is complete.

GREEK LEG OF LAMB

with HEIRLOOM TOMATO SALAD
AND FIELD CUKE TZATZIKI

Nova Scotia has amazing lamb, reared in the fields along the Northumberland Shore. We have become more familiar with authentic Greek food due in large part to the annual Greekfest in Halifax. This particular dish is great for entertaining on the back deck, and grilling the leg of lamb without the bone gives you some nice options. First, when marinating, it gives more surface area and helps develop flavour. Second, the leg can be separated into three pieces of different sizes, allowing for a range of doneness. And third, carving and presentation is simple and extremely elegant, but still casual enough to suit a backyard party. For the salad, I like to highlight my favourite summer ingredient here: heirloom tomatoes. I also use a very common Nova Scotia variety of field cucumber here instead of the English cucumber varietal, as I find them an under-appreciated summer vegetable.

LEG OF LAMB
INGREDIENTS

1 boneless leg lamb (about 4 lb/2 kg)

4 cloves garlic, minced

2 bay leaves

1 shallot, minced

1/2 cup (125 mL) red wine

1/4 cup (60 mL) Dijon mustard

1/4 cup (60 mL) liquid honey

1/4 cup (60 mL) extra-virgin olive oil

2 tbsp (30 mL) chopped fresh rosemary or thyme

2 tsp (10 mL) oregano

1/4 tsp (1 mL) pepper

Several dashes hot sauce

Zest and juice of 1 lemon

Salt and pepper to taste

Vegetable oil

Heirloom Tomato Salad (recipe follows)

Field Cuke Tzatziki (recipe follows)

METHOD

From lamb, trim and discard excess fat; transfer to resealable freezer bag. In bowl, whisk together garlic, bay leaves, shallot, wine, mustard, honey, oil, rosemary or thyme, oregano, pepper, hot sauce and lemon zest and juice; pour over lamb. Seal bag and massage lamb to coat. Refrigerate and let marinate for at least 3 hours or up to 12 hours.

Reserving marinade, drain lamb and pat dry with paper towels. Transfer reserved marinade to saucepan; bring to a boil and cook until thickened and reduced by half. Set aside.

Sprinkle lamb generously with salt and pepper; brush grill rack with oil to prevent sticking. Transfer lamb to grill; roast over very high heat, turning and basting with reserved marinade, until browned all over, about 5 minutes per side. Reduce temperature to medium and place lamb on top rack (ideal temperature for this stage is 275°F to 300°F (135°C to 150°C); checking internal-read thermometer, roast until thermometer registers 5° below desired doneness temperature (see chart, below), 15 to 40 minutes. Remove from heat; let stand for at least 30 minutes.

Rare	125°F (50°C) begin resting at 120°F
Medium-rare	130°F (55°C) begin resting at 125°F
Medium	140°F (60°C) begin resting at 135°F
Medium-well	150°F (65°C) begin resting at 145°F
Well-done	160°F (71°C) begin resting at 155°F

Thinly carve lamb and fan slices over Heirloom Tomato Salad. Serve Field Cuke Tzatziki as side dish.

Makes 8 full-supper servings

If your butcher has boned the lamb for you, all you need to do is trim away any excess fat. The meat from around the bone can be rolled up into a tied roast, but I usually cut it into 3 smaller pieces, with the 2 larger leg muscles being the main 2 roasts. This also allows me to do 3 different doneness levels (rare, medium or well) if I am serving several people.

HEIRLOOM TOMATO SALAD
INGREDIENTS
5 lb (2.2 kg) mixed heirloom tomatoes
2 tbsp (30 mL) coarse kosher salt
1/3 cup (75 mL) extra-virgin olive oil
1/4 cup (60 mL) red wine or sherry vinegar
1 cup (250 mL) fresh basil leaves

METHOD
Roughly cut tomatoes, slicing each colour into different shapes (slices, wedges, large dice, etc). Transfer to bowl and sprinkle with salt; toss to coat. Let stand for 20 to 30 minutes. Drain and discard excess moisture released by salt. On large serving platter, arrange tomato mixture; drizzle with oil and wine. Garnish with basil.

FIELD CUKE TZATZIKI
INGREDIENTS
1 field cucumber
1 tsp (5 mL) kosher salt
2 cloves garlic
2 cups (500 mL) plain Greek yoghurt
2 tbsp (30 mL) extra-virgin olive oil
1 tbsp (15 mL) chopped fresh dillweed
1/2 tsp (2 mL) hot sauce
Zest and juice of 1/2 lemon
Pepper to taste

METHOD
Peel cucumber, halve lengthwise; remove and discard seeds and soft pulp at centre. Grate cucumber into bowl; sprinkle with salt and toss to coat. Refrigerate for about 1 hour. Transfer to colander and squeeze out excess moisture released by salt; transfer to bowl. With microplane, grate garlic as finely as possible and add to cucumber mixture. Add yoghurt, oil, dillweed, hot sauce, lemon zest and juice and pepper; whisk to combine. Cover and refrigerate until ready to serve.

Makes 2 1/2 cups (625 mL)

FISHERMAN'S PLATTER
my way

*Nova Scotia seafood
fried three ways*

. . .

*sour cream and
chive mash*

. . .

*braised peas with leeks
and romaine*

. . .

bacon tartar sauce

FISHERMAN'S PLATTER *my way*
NOVA SCOTIA SEAFOOD FRIED THREE WAYS
with SOUR CREAM AND CHIVE MASH, BRAISED PEAS WITH LEEKS AND ROMAINE, *and* BACON TARTAR SAUCE

Whether you're visiting a fish shack on the boardwalk, dining on takeout on a blanket at the beach or enjoying a sit-down evening meal in a gastropub, summer seafood restaurants of all ranges offer a seafood platter. Beer-battered fish and shellfish served alongside fries and coleslaw is a delicious summer tradition. My elaborate spread is a twist on the classic seafood platter, with more vegetables on the side and a few new ways to prepare the fish. If you prefer, you can simply use beer batter or panko crust for everything and save some extra work. Think of this recipe as a list of possibilities and choose whatever makes sense to you. And — yes — you can even serve it with fries if you want!

BATTERED HADDOCK
INGREDIENTS

1 egg

1 ½ cups (375 mL) all-purpose flour, plus extra for dredging

½ cup (125 mL) cornstarch

1 tbsp (15 mL) baking powder

½ tsp (2 mL) salt

1 can (355 mL) beer

4 fillets fresh haddock (about 6 oz/175 g each) cut in half

Salt and pepper

When frying on a stovetop at home, choose a large steep-sided pot and place about 8 cups (2 L) of fresh vegetable oil in it, ensuring the oil does not fill more than 25 percent of the pot. Use a thermometer and heat the oil over medium heat until it registers 350ºF (180ºC). This is the ideal temperature for frying all of the seafood here. Each recipe simply requires a variation on the time the fish needs to stay in the oil.

METHOD

In bowl, whisk together egg, flour, cornstarch, baking powder and salt. Add beer, stirring until smooth batter forms. Pat haddock dry with paper towel, then sprinkle all over with salt and pepper. Sprinkle flour into wide shallow dish; dredge haddock in flour, shaking off excess, then dip into beer batter to coat. Cook haddock in the fry oil (see sidebar) until golden, about 4 minutes; with slotted spoon, transfer to paper towel to drain. Set aside and keep warm until ready to serve.

Makes 6 to 8 servings

PANKO CRUSTED SCALLOPS
INGREDIENTS

1 lb (500 g) sea scallops (10 to 20)
2 eggs, beaten
Salt and pepper to taste
1 cup (250 mL) panko bread crumbs
¼ cup (60 mL) all-purpose flour

METHOD

Remove small muscles from sides of scallops. Pour eggs into shallow dish; stir in salt and pepper. Pour bread crumbs into second shallow dish. Sprinkle flour into third shallow dish. Dredge scallops in flour, shaking off excess, then dip into eggs and roll in bread crumbs to coat. Cook scallops for 3 minutes in the fry oil (see sidebar). With slotted spoon, transfer to paper towel to drain. Set aside and keep warm until ready to serve.

Makes 6 to 8 servings

FRIED BUTTERMILK CLAMS
INGREDIENTS

16 freshly shucked soft-shell (steamer) clams
1 cup (250 mL) buttermilk
¼ tsp (1 mL) cayenne pepper
¼ tsp (1 mL) salt
2 cups (500 mL) corn flour
1 tsp (5 mL) Old Bay Seasoning

METHOD

Place clams in bowl; stir in buttermilk, cayenne pepper and salt. Cover and refrigerate for about 2 hours.

In second bowl, stir together corn flour and Old Bay Seasoning. Toss in reserved clams to coat. Drop each clam in fry oil (see sidebar) for about 2 minutes until golden and crispy. Remove from oil with a slotted spoon and drain on clean towels; season with salt and pepper if desired.

Makes 6 to 8 servings

SOUR CREAM AND CHIVE MASH
INGREDIENTS

3 lb (1.5 kg) new potatoes, unpeeled

1 tbsp (15 mL) sea salt

1 cup (250 mL) full-fat sour cream

½ cup (125 mL) butter

½ cup (125 mL) whole milk

¼ cup (60 mL) sliced fresh chives

Pepper to taste

METHOD

Halve small potatoes and quarter large ones; transfer to large pot and add salt and enough water to cover. Bring to a boil; cook until fork-tender. With colander, drain; let stand for about 5 minutes to steam dry. Return to pot.

With fork, stir in sour cream, butter, milk, chives and pepper, gently mashing into coarse mixture.

Makes 6 to 8 servings

For this recipe, lumps are good, so don't overwork the potatoes and leave plenty of whole pieces in the pot. The result will be a creamy base with lots of texture, as well.

BRAISED PEAS WITH LEEKS AND ROMAINE
INGREDIENTS

1 small head romaine lettuce, stem end removed

2 tbsp (30 mL) extra-virgin olive oil

1 large leek, thinly sliced

1 clove garlic, finely chopped

½ tsp (2 mL) salt

1 lb (500 g) freshly shucked sweet peas

1 cup (250 mL) vegetable stock

¼ cup (60 mL) chopped fresh mint

2 tbsp (30 mL) butter

Pepper to taste

METHOD

Remove and discard damaged or discoloured leaves from romaine; separate remaining leaves, then remove and discard leaf spines. Coarsely chop leaves into 2-inch (5 cm) lengths; set aside.

In saucepan over medium-high heat, warm oil; sauté leek, garlic and salt until vegetables have softened. Add peas and vegetable stock; cover, bring to a boil and cook for 2 minutes. Stir in lettuce; cook, uncovered, until almost all of the liquid has evaporated, 3 to 5 minutes. Remove from heat; stir in mint, butter and pepper.

Makes 6 to 8 servings

BACON TARTAR SAUCE
INGREDIENTS

6 strips smoky bacon, finely chopped

1 cup (250 mL) mayonnaise

¼ cup (60 mL) green relish or finely chopped gherkins

1 tbsp (15 mL) Dijon mustard

1 tbsp (15 mL) capers, finely chopped

2 tsp (10 mL) lemon juice

1 tsp (5 mL) hot sauce

METHOD

In saucepan over medium heat, cook bacon until crisp and browned. Transfer to paper towel to drain. In bowl, stir together mayonnaise, relish, mustard, capers, lemon juice and hot sauce; stir in bacon.

Makes 2 cups (500 mL)

BARBECUED MACKEREL
WITH QUICK SWEET CHILI GREEN TOMATO CHOW

My mother served us fried mackerel every fall after the mackerel runs in late August and early September ended in her hometown of River Bourgeois, Cape Breton, where I spent many of my childhood summers. My grandfather, uncle, father, brother and I used to head out from False Bay in a small aluminium boat at dawn, motor past Phillips Rocks and into St. Peters Bay. There is really nothing like hitting a school of mackerel on the open water and jigging for them with a hand-held line — unparalleled excitement for a 12-year-old boy! I can still remember my mother dusting the mackerel in flour before pan-frying it for a lunch with boiled potatoes and chow. My version is a little different — it grills the fish whole — and works best if you use a fish basket to hold the mackerel while grilling. You can easily buy chow at a farmers' market, but this spicy green tomato "pan pickle" can be made quickly and easily on the side burner of your gas barbecue as the fish cooks.

INGREDIENTS

4 whole (with heads) mackerel, drawn and cleaned
¼ cup (60 mL) extra-virgin olive oil
Salt and pepper
4 green tomatoes, diced
3 green onions, finely sliced
2 cloves garlic, finely chopped
1 red chili pepper, seeded and finely minced
3 tbsp (45 mL) liquid honey
3 tbsp (45 mL) chopped fresh cilantro
2 tbsp (30 mL) finely chopped gingerroot
2 tsp (10 mL) soy sauce
1 tsp (5 mL) sesame oil
1 tsp (5 mL) fish sauce
Zest and juice of 2 limes

METHOD

With tip of sharp knife, cut several ¼-inch (5 mm) deep slits into sides of mackerel. Drizzle all over with 2 tbsp (30 mL) of the olive oil, then sprinkle with salt and pepper; transfer to fish basket. Transfer to grill set on medium-high; cook, turning once halfway through, until fish flakes easily with fork, about 8 minutes. Keep warm until ready to serve.

In large saucepan over high heat, warm remaining olive oil until beginning to smoke; sauté tomatoes for 2 minutes. Stir in onions, garlic, chili pepper, honey, cilantro, gingerroot, soy sauce, sesame oil, fish sauce, and lime zest and juice; bring to a boil and cook for 4 to 5 minutes. Serve this chow with reserved mackerel.

Makes 4 to 6 servings, including 2 cups (500 mL) chow

When you're cooking the chow, a lot of juice comes out of the tomatoes, but that's fine — the resulting sauce will season the mackerel perfectly. You can adjust the seasonings with a little salt or pepper and serve it hot over the fish. Alternatively, you can make it ahead of time and serve it cold as you would a traditional green tomato chow. This accompaniment is also delicious with other fish, seafood and sausages.

LOBSTER
and SWEET PEA
RISOTTO

Being a chef in Nova Scotia has its perks for sure, and having the freshest lobster available year-round is one of them. Although the simplest preparations are often best for lobster, it is rather versatile and allows for some creativity too. This is a signature lobster dish of mine, but also one that captures the essence of a summer garden: sweet peas out of the shell. Risotto continues to be one of the most desired dishes on restaurant menus, and home cooks are not nearly as intimidated as they once were to dive in and try making it themselves. For a real boost of flavour, take the time to make the lobster broth if you can, but if you just can't manage it, chicken broth is fine too.

LOBSTER AND SWEET PEA RISOTTO
INGREDIENTS
¼ cup (60 mL) butter, plus 2 tbsp/30 mL for finishing risotto

2 shallots, minced

1 stalk celery, minced

¼ fennel bulb, minced

½ tsp (2 mL) sea salt

½ tsp (2 mL) pepper

1 cup (250 mL) arborio or carnaroli rice

½ cup (125 mL) white wine

4 cups (1 L) Lobster Broth (recipe follows)

¾ cup (175 mL) fresh sweet peas

2 cups (500 mL) chunked cooked lobster meat (about 2 lobsters)

½ cup (125 mL) creamy goat cheese

¼ cup (60 mL) grated Parmesan cheese

¼ cup (60 mL) sliced fresh chives

METHOD
In saucepan over medium heat, melt ¼ cup (60 mL) butter; sauté shallots, celery, fennel, salt and pepper until vegetables are softened and translucent, about 5 minutes. Stir in rice; cook, stirring, until rice is translucent, about 3 minutes. Stir in wine; cook, stirring, until liquid is absorbed. One ladle at a time, add Lobster Broth and cook, stirring constantly. When half the broth has been added, add the peas to the pot. Add the remaining broth to the pot and cook, stirring, for about 14 to 15 minutes.

Stir in lobster meat; cook until rice is tender but still el dente, 1 to 4 minutes. Stir in goat cheese, Parmesan and remaining 2 tbsp/30 mL butter. Remove heat; let stand for 3 to 5 minutes. Add chives.

Makes 6 to 8 servings

LOBSTER BROTH
1 cooked lobster

5 cups (1.25 L) chicken or vegetable stock

1 cup water

METHOD
Remove meat from lobster; set aside for Lobster and Sweet Pea Risotto (recipe above). Break shells into small pieces; add to stockpot along with chicken stock and water and simmer for 1 hour.

In batches, transfer to blender; pulse together shells and stock until thickened and pea-sized pieces of shells remain; through cheesecloth-lined sieve, strain and discard solids. Return stock to pot; keep warm until ready to use for risotto.

PEACH AND RASPBERRY GRUNT
with HONEY VANILLA ICE CREAM

There's a special flavour to a peach picked from a familiar orchard. My favourites are the peaches my father grows in his Port Williams orchard, so the idea for this dish started in his backyard. Coupe Melba (named after opera-singer Nellie Melba) is a forgotten classic that reminds me of my apprenticeship at the Savoy Hotel in London, the kitchen where chef Auguste Escoffier created this dessert for the famous diva. Blueberry grunt, a long-standing Nova Scotia dessert, is one of my favourites as well, but this new way to enjoy valley peaches pays tribute to some flavour combinations that just work well. Escoffier knew what he was doing and so does my dad.

PEACH AND RASPBERRY GRUNT
INGREDIENTS

8 ripe peaches
1/3 cup (75 mL) granulated sugar
3 tbsp (45 mL) butter
1 tsp (5 mL) vanilla extract
1/4 tsp (1 mL) nutmeg
3/4 cup (175 mL) white wine
1 cup (250 mL) all-purpose flour
1 tbsp (15 mL) plus 1 tsp (5 mL) granulated sugar
2 tsp (10 mL) baking powder
1/4 tsp (1 mL) salt
3 tbsp (45 mL) butter, cold and diced
2 tbsp (30 mL) shortening
1 egg
1/2 cup (125 mL) whole milk
Honey Vanilla Ice Cream (recipe follows)
Raspberries
Raspberry Sauce (recipe follows)

METHOD

Halve peaches, remove and discard pits; cut into irregular chunks; set aside. In wide shallow saucepan or skillet with tight-fitting lid over medium-high heat, stir together 1/3 cup (75 mL) sugar, butter, vanilla and nutmeg; cook until butter has melted. Stir in reserved peaches and wine; cover and bring to a boil. Cook until peaches release juice, 1 to 2 minutes.

Into bowl, sift together flour, 1 tbsp (15 mL) sugar, baking powder and salt. Using 2 knives or pastry cutter, cut in butter and shortening until mixture resembles coarse meal. In second bowl, beat together egg and milk; with wooden spoon, stir into flour mixture until stiff batter forms.

With hands, form batter into 6 balls; drop into simmering peach mixture, gently pushing down to surround with fruit and sauce. Cover and gently simmer for 15 minutes. Serve warm with scoop Honey Vanilla Ice Cream, raspberries and Raspberry Sauce.

Makes 6 portions

HONEY VANILLA ICE CREAM
INGREDIENTS
2 cups (500 mL) heavy cream (35% mf)
2 cups (500 mL) whole milk
½ cup (125 mL) liquid honey
2 vanilla pods, split lengthwise
4 egg yolks
¼ cup (60 mL) granulated sugar
Pinch salt

METHOD
In saucepan, stir together cream, milk and honey. Scrape vanilla seeds into pan and add pods; bring to a boil. Immediately reduce heat to low; gently simmer for 10 minutes. Remove from heat; set aside.

In heatproof bowl, whisk together egg yolks, sugar and salt until light and smooth. One ladle at a time, stir reserved cream mixture into egg mixture until blended. Set bowl over pot of simmering water; gently cook, stirring constantly with spatula until thickened enough to coat back of spoon. Set bowl in larger bowl filled with ice water; let cool. With slotted spoon, remove and discard vanilla pods. Cover and refrigerate custard until cold, about 1 hour. Transfer to electric ice cream maker and churn following manufacturer's instructions. Transfer to airtight container and freeze for at least 2 hours before serving.

Makes 6 cups (1 ½ L)

RASPBERRY SAUCE
INGREDIENTS
2 ½ cups (625 mL) fresh or frozen raspberries
⅓ cup (75 mL) granulated sugar
⅓ cup (75 mL) water
Juice of ½ lemon

METHOD
In saucepan, stir together raspberries, sugar and water; bring to a simmer. Immediately transfer to blender; purée until blended and smooth. Through fine-mesh sieve, strain into bowl. Stir in lemon juice. Transfer to airtight container and refrigerate until ready to use.

STRAWBERRY SHORTCAKE

with CREAM SCONES

AND WHITE CHOCOLATE WHIPPED CREAM

It only feels like summer in Nova Scotia once you've eaten your first strawberry shortcake. This is a recipe that I feel modernizes the dessert a bit by adding some melted white chocolate to the whipped cream and a simple wine glaze on the fresh berries. Feel free to use a standard tea biscuit here, as would be the traditional way served in homes, family restaurants and church suppers around the province. But my friend Brady makes the best cream scone I've ever had, and that's coming from a guy who helped produce the famed Savoy Hotel afternoon tea during his apprenticeship in London! I highly recommend giving them a try for a great twist on a summer classic.

STRAWBERRY GLAZE AND WHIPPED CREAM
INGREDIENTS

3 market quarts (3 L) strawberries, hulled and halved

¾ cup (175 mL) red wine

⅓ cup (75 mL) granulated sugar

2 tbsp (30 mL) water

1 tsp (5 mL) vanilla extract

Pinch salt

½ tsp (2 mL) lemon juice

½ cup (125 mL) chopped white chocolate

2 cups (500 mL) heavy cream (35% mf)

2 tbsp (30 mL) crème de cacao

8 Cream Scones (recipe follows)

METHOD

Transfer 2 quarts (2 L) strawberries to bowl; cover and refrigerate until ready to use.

In saucepan, bring wine to a boil; cook for 1 minute. Stir in remaining strawberries, sugar, water, vanilla and salt; reduce heat and simmer, stirring occasionally, until strawberries have softened into sauce, about 10 minutes. Transfer to blender; purée until blended and smooth. Through fine-mesh sieve, strain, discarding solids. Transfer glaze to airtight container, stir in lemon juice; cover and refrigerate until ready to use.

Place chocolate in small heatproof bowl; place over pot of simmering water. With spatula, gently stir until melted, smooth and glossy. Remove from heat; let stand until room temperature.

In bowl, beat together cream and crème de cacao until in soft peaks and doubled in volume. With whisk attachment and medium speed, and adding reserved chocolate mixture in slow, steady stream, beat chocolate into cream mixture for about 20 seconds, then increase speed to high and beat for about 5 seconds (small balls of chocolate may still be visible in mixture).

Pour half of the reserved glaze over reserved strawberries; toss to coat (if glaze is too thick, stir in a small amount of water).

Make vertical slice partway through each Cream Scone; open slightly. Evenly divide strawberry mixture among scones. Top with whipped cream and drizzle with any remaining glaze.

Makes 8 individual shortcakes

* A few notes on making the white chocolate whipped cream: in order for the chocolate to become incorporated into the whipping cream, it must be still viscous but not terribly hot, as this will cause the cream to collapse. As long as the chocolate doesn't feel warm to the touch, you should be fine to begin. Also, small little lumps of chocolate may remain in the cream sometimes, but they melt when you eat it and give an interesting texture to the dish, so don't fret too much if the cream isn't perfectly smooth.

CREAM SCONES
INGREDIENTS

2 cups (500 mL) sifted all-purpose flour

1 tbsp (15 mL) baking powder

1 tbsp (15 mL) granulated sugar

½ tsp (2 mL) salt

½ cup (125 mL) butter, diced

1 egg

¾ cup (175 mL) heavy cream (35% mf)

1 tbsp (15 mL) icing sugar

METHOD

In bowl, whisk together flour, baking powder, sugar and salt; with fingers, rub in butter until mixture has pea-sized bits. In glass measure, with fork, lightly beat egg; add enough cream to fill 1 cup (250 mL). Stir into flour mixture just until dough comes together (do not overwork or knead). Discarding any flour in bottom of bowl, transfer dough to lightly floured surface. Pat into circle about 1-inch (2.5 cm) thick; cut into 8 wedges. Transfer to parchment paper–lined baking sheet, at least 2 inches (5 cm) apart. Bake in 400°F (200°C) oven until lightweight and golden on edges, about 12 minutes. Through small fine-meshed sieve, sprinkle icing sugar overtop.

Butter-Blitzed Celery Root and Chanterelle Soup
page 84

OYSTERS ON THE 1/2 WITH HONEY MIGNONETTE, SMOKED MACKEREL
AND APPLE SLAW, G & T GRANITA, CHIPOTLE "KETCHUP," GARDEN
VINAIGRETTE AND CHARRED-ONION RELISH

SQUASH AND APPLE SOUP WITH SMOKY BACON CROUTONS

MUSSELS NORMANDY

CREAM OF TOMATO SOUP AND OATMEAL BROWN BREAD
GRILLED CHEESE

BUTTER-BLITZED CELERY ROOT AND CHANTERELLE SOUP

AUTUMN

CRAZY-GOOD MAC AND CHEESE

SUNDAY PRIME RIB ROAST WITH SIMPLE PAN GRAVY
AND SKILLET POTATO GRATIN

HARVEST BRUSCHETTA: ROAST FIELD TOMATOES AND BASIL WITH AGED
GOUDA, CREAMED CHANTERELLES WITH SAGE AND GRILLED PEAR
WITH BLUE CHEESE AND CIDER VINEGAR HONEY

PEAR GINGERBREAD CAKE WITH DULCE DE LECHE AND CHANTILLY CREAM

PUMPKIN MOUSSE TORTE WITH GINGERSNAP CRUST, SPICED PUMPKIN
PRALINE, ORANGE CRANBERRY JAM SAUCE AND CHANTILLY CREAM

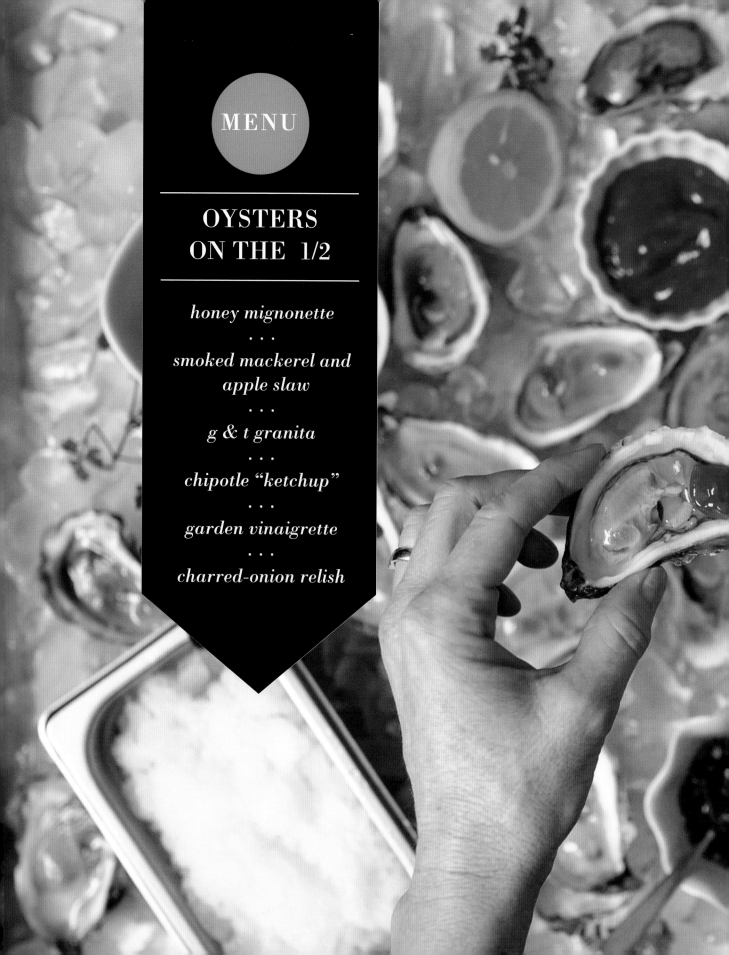

MENU

OYSTERS ON THE 1/2

honey mignonette

. . .

smoked mackerel and apple slaw

. . .

g & t granita

. . .

chipotle "ketchup"

. . .

garden vinaigrette

. . .

charred-onion relish

OYSTERS ON THE 1/2
WITH HONEY MIGNONETTE, SMOKED MACKEREL *and* APPLE SLAW, G & T GRANITA,
CHIPOTLE "KETCHUP", GARDEN VINAIGRETTE AND CHARRED-ONION RELISH

For decades, oysters have been cultivated in Nova Scotia, and now there are about 40 farms along the coast. Each body of water affects the flavour of the oysters, resulting in friendly regional rivalries between farmers. I may have my favourites, but I love and respect every single farmer for cultivating these for my kitchen. I considered many different oyster dishes for this book, but – really – freshly shucked oysters are perfect and ultimately what most connoisseurs want. My garnishes include some familiar recipes and a few new ones I've created. To entertain a large group, set up your very own oyster bar on your back deck or kitchen table. Make one, two or all of these garnishes, then start shucking! You can buy oysters in small, medium or large (choice) sizes. I usually estimate about three per person if throwing a party, but maybe more if I know the crowd are oyster lovers.

To serve oysters, you'll need some towels and at least one oyster knife. Opening oysters can take a bit of practice, but generally, you need to secure the oyster in a folded towel with the hinge-end exposed. Insert the knife into the joint and press down firmly, then twist. You will feel the hinge pop out. Then run the knife along the top of the shell inside, separating the muscle and keeping the meat in tact. Remove the top of the shell, and then slide the knife under the oyster, releasing the meat from the bottom muscle. It's that easy!

HONEY MIGNONETTE
INGREDIENTS
¼ cup (60 mL) liquid honey
¼ cup (60 mL) sherry wine vinegar
¼ cup (60 mL) white wine vinegar
2 tbsp (30 mL) finely chopped shallots
½ tsp (2 mL) crushed peppercorns
Pinch salt

METHOD
In small bowl, stir together honey, sherry wine vinegar, white wine vinegar, shallots, peppercorns and salt, until honey has dissolved; let stand for 30 minutes. Stir again just before serving.

Makes 1 cup (250 mL)

SMOKED MACKEREL AND APPLE SLAW
INGREDIENTS
1 fillet smoked mackerel (about 3 ounces/90 g), skin removed
1 small tart apple, unpeeled
2 green onions, finely chopped
2 tbsp (30 mL) extra-virgin olive oil
½ tsp (2 mL) Dijon mustard
Zest and juice of ½ lemon
Salt and pepper to taste

METHOD
Carefully removing bones from belly section, pull mackerel flesh into small flakes; transfer to small bowl. Core apple; cut into ¹⁄₁₆-inch (1 mm) rounds, then julienne and add to mackerel. Add green onions and toss together.

In second bowl, whisk together oil, mustard, lemon zest and juice, salt and pepper; pour over mackerel mixture. Without breaking up julienned apple, gently toss with fingers.

Makes 2 cups (500 mL)

G & T GRANITA
INGREDIENTS

¼ cup (60 mL) granulated sugar
¼ cup (60 mL) water
2 cups (500 mL) tonic water
½ cup (125 mL) gin
Juice of 2 limes
2 tbsp (30 mL) finely sliced fresh mint leaves
¼ English cucumber (optional)

METHOD

In saucepan over high heat, stir together sugar and water until sugar
has dissolved and mixture is syrupy. Remove from heat; let cool to
room temperature. Stir in tonic water, gin and lime juice; pour into wide
shallow dish. Freeze for 1 hour; whisk in mint leaves. Return to freezer
for 1 hour; whisk again. Return to freezer for 1 hour; whisk again. Return
to freezer for 30 minutes; with fork, scrape granita into frosty texture,
keeping it in the freezer until ready to serve. If desired, halve cucumber,
seed and finely dice. Top each oyster with about 1 tsp (5 mL) G & T
Granita, then, if desired, garnish with sprinkle of cucumber.

Makes 2 cups (500 mL)

CHIPOTLE "KETCHUP"
INGREDIENTS

4 ripe tomatoes

2 tbsp (30 mL) canola oil

2 cloves garlic, sliced

1 onion, finely chopped

1/2 sweet red pepper, finely chopped

1 tbsp (15 mL) smoked paprika

3 tbsp (45 mL) finely chopped chipotle peppers in adobo sauce

2 tbsp (30 mL) tomato paste

3 tbsp (45 mL) packed brown sugar

2 tbsp (30 mL) red wine vinegar

1/2 tsp (2 mL) salt

1/4 tsp (1 mL) ground cloves

1/4 tsp (1 mL) ground allspice

METHOD

Bring large pot of water to a boil; fill large bowl with water and a few ice cubes. Trim and discard stem ends from tomatoes; with tip of knife, cut small X in bottom of each. With tongs, plunge each tomato into boiling water for 10 seconds; immediately plunge into ice water. With paring knife, peel off and discard skins. Halve each widthwise; squeeze out and discard seeds and pulp. Finely chop remaining firm flesh to make tomato concassé and transfer to small bowl; set aside.

In small saucepan over medium-high heat, warm oil; sauté garlic, onion and red pepper until lightly browned and beginning to caramelize, about 10 minutes. Stir in paprika and cook for 2 to 3 minutes. Stir in chipotle peppers with sauce and tomato paste and cook for 2 to 3 minutes. Stir in reserved concassé, brown sugar, vinegar, salt, cloves and allspice. Reduce heat to medium-low and bring to a simmer; cook, uncovered and stirring occasionally, until thickened to consistency of applesauce, 30 to 45 minutes. Remove from heat; let cool completely. Top oysters with about 1/4 teaspoon as a garnish.

Makes 1 cup (250 mL)

GARDEN VINAIGRETTE
INGREDIENTS

1/2 small red onion, coarsely chopped

1/2 sweet red pepper, coarsely chopped

1/2 sweet green pepper, coarsely chopped

1/2 tsp (2 mL) salt

2 anchovy fillets

2 cloves garlic

1 tbsp (15 mL) capers

1 tsp (5 mL) granulated sugar

3 tbsp (45 mL) extra-virgin olive oil

2 tsp (10 mL) red wine vinegar

Juice of 1 lemon

Dash Tabasco sauce

1 ripe tomato, unpeeled, stem end removed

5 to 6 fresh basil leaves, finely sliced

3 tbsp (45 mL) chopped parsley

Pepper to taste

METHOD

In food processor, pulse together onion, red pepper, green pepper and salt until finely chopped (don't purée); transfer to cheesecloth-lined bowl. Gather corners of cheesecloth and squeeze liquid into bowl. Discard liquid; transfer solids to second bowl and set aside.

In mortar, combine anchovy, garlic, capers and sugar; with pestle, smash together until smooth purée. Add oil, vinegar, lemon juice and Tabasco sauce, mixing well. With box grater, grate tomato into anchovy mixture. With fork, stir in basil, parsley and pepper. Stir anchovy mixture into onion mixture; let stand for at least 2 hours or even overnight. Top each oyster with about 1 tsp (5 mL).

Makes 1 1/2 cups (375 mL)

CHARRED-ONION RELISH
INGREDIENTS

1 large Vidalia onion, sliced in ¼-inch (5 mm) rounds
2 tbsp (30 mL) extra-virgin olive oil
3 tbsp (45 mL) white balsamic vinegar
2 tbsp (30 mL) chopped fresh chives
1 tbsp (15 mL) granulated sugar
Salt and pepper to taste

METHOD

Preheat grill to high; thoroughly clean rack. Brush onion slices with 1 tbsp (15 mL) of the oil; transfer to rack and grill, covered and without touching for at least 5 minutes, until well charred on bottom. With spatula, gently transfer to tray; let cool enough to handle. Finely chop into irregular dice and transfer to bowl. Stir in remaining oil, vinegar, chives, sugar and salt and pepper until sugar has dissolved; cover and refrigerate for at least 12 hours. Top each oyster with about ½ tsp (2 mL) relish.

Makes 1 ½ cups (375 mL)

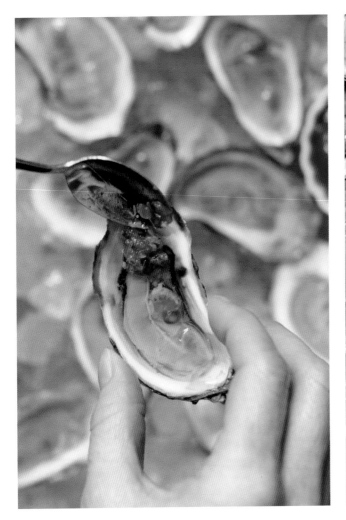

SQUASH AND APPLE SOUP
with SMOKY BACON CROUTONS

For me, this recipe embodies harvest time on my parents' property in Port Williams. Now, I grow my own squash. Adding in apples from Dad's orchard seemed like the natural thing to do. I have to say that the smokiness and crunch of the bacon *croutons really take this dish to another level. For a vegetarian version, you can omit them or try topping each serving with toasted pumpkin seeds, a crumble of blue cheese or a few drops of balsamic vinegar.*

SQUASH AND APPLE SOUP
INGREDIENTS

4 cups (1 L) coarsely chopped butternut squash
4 cups (1 L) coarsely chopped buttercup squash
2 cups (500 mL) coarsely chopped onions
2 cups (500 mL) sliced cored unpeeled apples
1 cup (250 mL) coarsely chopped celery
⅓ cup (75 mL) extra-virgin olive oil
8 cups (2 L) low-sodium chicken or vegetable stock
1 pod star anise
1 cup (250 mL) apple cider
1 tsp (5 mL) cinnamon
1 tsp (5 mL) salt
1 tsp (5 mL) pepper
1 cup (250 mL) heavy cream (35% mf)
Smoky Bacon Croutons (recipe follows)

METHOD

In large bowl, toss together butternut squash, buttercup squash, onions, apples, celery and oil to coat. Evenly spread in single layer on rimmed baking sheet; bake in 400°F (220°C) oven until squash and onions are caramelized and golden, about 20 minutes.

Transfer to stockpot over medium-high heat; add chicken stock, star anise, cider, cinnamon, salt and pepper; simmer for 1 hour. In batches, transfer to blender and purée; pass through a fine-meshed sieve, strain into bowl. Return stock to pot and stir in cream; bring just to a boil before serving. Garnish individual servings with Smoky Bacon Croutons.

Makes 6 lunch or appetizer servings

SMOKY BACON CROUTONS
INGREDIENTS

1 tbsp (15 mL) butter
3 slices double-smoked bacon, cut in ½-inch (5 cm) lengths
2 cups (500 mL) coarsely torn or diced crusty bread
1 tbsp (15 mL) chopped parsley

METHOD

In small cast-iron skillet over medium-high heat, melt butter; sauté bacon until crisp and browned. With slotted spoon, transfer to paper towel to drain. Add bread to pan; sauté until coated with fat and beginning to smoke. Transfer pan to 350°F (180°C) oven and bake until golden brown, about 5 minutes. Remove from oven; toss in reserved bacon and parsley.

MUSSELS NORMANDY

There's a good reason that mussels are a standard appetizer in Nova Scotia. Simply steamed and dipped in butter or topped with one of the many sauces that show up on creative menus, sweet and briny mussels stand the test of time. I'm a fan of this recipe that also showcases local fall apples, along with shallots, butter, rosemary and full cream. The smell reminds me of a dish from Northern France, hence the name — and my suggestion that you serve it with a chewy homemade baguette that you can tear up by hand, as though you're in a French bistro by the sea. The sauce is too good to waste a drop, so use the bread for dipping!

INGREDIENTS

2 lb (1 kg) fresh mussels
1 tart apple, such as Honeycrisp
2 tbsp (30 mL) butter
1 clove garlic, minced
2 tbsp (30 mL) finely chopped shallots
½ cup (125 mL) dry sparkling apple cider
Pinch each salt and pepper
¾ cup (175 mL) heavy cream (35% mf)
1 tbsp (15 mL) chopped fresh rosemary
1 tbsp (15 mL) chopped parsley
2 green onions (green parts only), sliced

METHOD

Under cold running water, scrub and de-beard mussels, discarding any that are damaged or don't close when lightly tapped; set aside. Julienne apple; set aside.

In saucepan large enough to accommodate mussels, melt butter; sauté garlic and shallots until translucent. Add cider, salt, pepper and reserved mussels; cover and let steam until mussels have opened, 5 to 7 minutes. With slotted spoon and discarding any unopened mussels, transfer mussels to warmed individual serving bowls; cover and keep warm.

Stir cream, rosemary and parsley into cooking liquid in pan; bring to a rapid boil and cook until liquid is reduced by half. Stir in apple and green onions; cook for 1 minute. Spoon over mussels.

Makes 4 appetizer portions or 2 entrée portions

CREAM OF TOMATO SOUP
and OATMEAL BROWN BREAD GRILLED CHEESE

This is comfort food at its finest and one of my favourite meals on earth. Knowing this, Jacqueline (my fiancée and the lady to whom this book is dedicated) made me this for dinner on the first of my birthdays we spent together. She couldn't have given me a better birthday supper! Naturally,

I recommend choosing a really good, local aged Cheddar. The oatmeal brown porridge bread makes the meal so delectably Nova Scotian that it may remind everyone of their childhood or maybe, like me, their birthday!

CREAM OF TOMATO SOUP
INGREDIENTS

3 lb (1.5 kg) ripe tomatoes

1 tbsp (15 mL) granulated sugar

2 tsp (10 mL) basil

2 tsp (10 mL) oregano

1 tsp (5 mL) kosher salt

1 tsp (5 mL) hot pepper flakes

¼ cup (125 mL) olive oil

6 cloves garlic, halved

1 large onion, sliced

1 can (4 oz/120 mL) tomato paste

3 cups (750 mL) vegetable stock

2 cups (500 mL) tomato juice

1 cup (250 mL) packed fresh basil leaves

1 cup (250 mL) heavy cream (35% mf)

Salt and pepper to taste

METHOD

Halve each tomato widthwise; arrange in single layer, cut-side up, on parchment paper–lined, rimmed baking sheet. In small bowl, stir together sugar, basil, oregano, salt and hot pepper flakes; evenly sprinkle over the tomatoes. Bake in 400°F (200°C) oven until beginning to caramelize, 30 to 40 minutes.

Meanwhile, in stockpot over medium-high heat, warm oil; sauté garlic and onion until onion begins to brown. Reduce heat to medium and stir in tomato paste; cook for 3 minutes. Stir in vegetable stock, tomato juice, basil leaves and tomatoes; simmer for 30 minutes. With immersion blender, purée (if smoother texture is desired, strain through sieve or colander and discard any solids). Return to pot; just before serving, stir in cream, salt and pepper and bring to a boil to rewarm.

Makes 8 to 10 servings

GRILLED CHEESE SANDWICH
INGREDIENTS

2 tsp (10 mL) butter, softened

2 slices Oatmeal Brown Bread, ½-inch (1 cm) thick (recipe follows)

½ cup (125 mL) aged Cheddar, shredded

METHOD

Spread butter over both sides of each slice. Evenly sprinkle Cheddar over 1 slice; top with remaining slice. In skillet over medium-low heat, cook until cheese is melted and bread is crisp and golden, 5 to 6 minutes per side.

When making a grilled cheese, soft butter is important, so it can be spread in a very thin, even layer over each entire slice of bread. The bread thickness is also key, so the ratio per bite of bread and cheese is right. I recommend ½-inch (1 cm) slices as this bread is quite dense and so delicious on its own. You can use sliced cheese, but I prefer shredding the cheese, as it melts more evenly, and sometimes, you get little bits of fried cheese on the edges as it cooks, an extra-tasty treat. Finally, "low and slow" is the most important thing to remember. Don't rush this process. Keep the pan on medium-low heat and watch it closely. If the pan is too hot, the bread will burn and the cheese in the middle will not melt. The recipe above is for one sandwich, so simply adjust quantities for the number of sandwiches you wish to make.

OATMEAL BROWN BREAD

This recipe was given to me by Don Gordon, a friend who has been making this bread for decades. He was given the recipe in 1966 by a family friend named Clara Oxner, who lived in Chester. Dense and delicious, this bread is a country-style treat that any home cook in the Maritimes could rightfully boast about.

INGREDIENTS

2 cups (500 mL) hot water
1 cup (250 mL) large-flake rolled oats
¼ cup (60 mL) packed brown sugar
1 tbsp (15 mL) active dry yeast
5 to 6 cups (1.25 to 1.5 L) all-purpose flour
½ cup (125 mL) cornmeal
1 tbsp (15 mL) salt
½ cup (125 mL) molasses
2 tbsp (30 mL) vegetable oil

METHOD

In large bowl, stir together water and oats; let stand just until lukewarm. Stir in brown sugar and yeast; let stand for 10 to 15 minutes. In second large bowl, whisk together flour, cornmeal and salt; add to oat mixture along with molasses and oil.

   With a wooden spoon, stir until dough is neither too wet nor too dry. On lightly floured surface, knead until dough is firm and elastic. Transfer to bowl, cover and let rise in warm draft-free spot until doubled in size. Transfer to lightly floured surface; with heel of hand, knock down dough, then halve and shape into two loaves. Transfer each to greased loaf pan, cover and let rise until doubled in size. Bake in centre of 375°F (190°C) oven until loaf sounds hollow when tapped on bottom, 30 to 40 minutes.

Makes 2 loaves

BUTTER-BLITZED CELERY ROOT
and CHANTERELLE SOUP

A good rule? Exceedingly simple recipes require exceptionally flavourful ingredients. As summer winds down, foragers begin poking their heads into our kitchens to sell us fresh chanterelle mushrooms. Around the same time, our farmers show up with their first crop of celery root. Beautiful *chanterelle mushrooms sautéed in butter are hard to beat, and the earthy flavour of celery root in this buttery soup is magical. I've added a unique twist by puréeing whole butter into it before serving, instead of stirring in cream. This aerates the broth and creates an amazing mouth feel.*

INGREDIENTS

6 cloves garlic, halved
6 cups (1.5 L) chicken stock
6 cups (1.5 L) diced celery root
2 cups (500 mL) whole milk or half-and-half cream (10% mf)
1 cup (250 mL) diced celery
1 cup (250 mL) diced onions
Salt and pepper to taste
1 tsp (5 mL) fenugreek seeds (optional)
1 cup (250 mL) cold butter, cubed in 1/2-inch (1 cm) pieces
8 oz (250 g) chanterelle mushrooms
1 tsp (5 mL) chopped fresh sage

METHOD

In stockpot over medium-high heat, stir together garlic, chicken stock, celery root, milk, celery, onions, salt, pepper and, if desired, fenugreek seeds; simmer until vegetables are falling apart, about 1 hour. Purée and strain through fine-meshed sieve or colander into a clean pot; set pot on a very low simmer to keep warm.

Before serving, reheat soup almost to boiling; in batches, transfer to high-speed blender, filling blender halfway each time; with centre cap of lid removed, place lid on blender and cover with tea towel, then begin blending on low, dropping 3 or 4 cubes of butter into batch, then finishing on high for 10 seconds. Transfer to individual warmed serving bowls.

While you are puréeing the soup, begin the mushrooms. In small skillet over medium-high heat, melt reserved butter; sauté mushrooms, salt and pepper until mushrooms are softened, stir in sage. Garnish each serving of soup with sautéed mushrooms in the middle of the bowl.

Makes 8 to 10 servings

CRAZY-GOOD MAC *and* CHEESE

It's hard to imagine a childhood without macaroni and cheese. We all have our own idea of the best version (usually your mother's), but I wanted to incorporate certain things into my "ultimate" recipe. A creamy mac and cheese should have visible macaroni noodles and not be a solid brick of mushy starch. There needs to be lots of flavour from some of my favourite local artisanal cheeses, and a tangy zip to balance the richness. And there needs to be a golden, crunchy crust on top. After several tries, I found that a classic Mornay sauce with the addition of some store-bought Velveeta cheese (yes, you read that correctly) gave me the texture and balance that I desired. So, here it is. Make modifications if you like, but I feel confident that mac and cheese lovers will find this quite appealing.

INGREDIENTS

1 lb (500 g) elbow macaroni

1/3 cup (75 mL) butter

1 small onion, minced

1/2 tsp (2 mL) salt

1/2 tsp (2 mL) pepper

1/4 cup (60 mL) plus 1 tbsp (15 mL) all-purpose flour

3 cups (750 mL) milk

2 cups (500 mL) half-and-half cream (10% mf)

2 tbsp (30 mL) Dijon mustard

1 tbsp (15 mL) Worcestershire sauce

1 tbsp (15 mL) hot sauce, such as Tabasco sauce or Sriracha

1/2 tsp (2 mL) nutmeg

1 package (1 lb/500 g) Velveeta cheese

2 cups (500 mL) shredded Gruyère cheese

2 cups (500 mL) grated aged Cheddar or Gouda cheese

1 1/2 cups (375 mL) grated Parmesan cheese

1/4 cup (60 mL) melted butter

1/2 cup (125 mL) fresh bread crumbs

1/2 cup (125 mL) crushed crackers, such as Saltines, Breton or Carr's Table Water

METHOD

In large pot of boiling salted water, cook macaroni until firm to bite but about three-quarters cooked, 5 to 6 minutes. Transfer to colander and drain under cold running water; set aside.

In large saucepan over medium-high heat, melt butter and cook until bubbling; sauté onion, salt and pepper until onions are translucent, about 3 minutes. Stir in flour until incorporated. Gently whisk in milk, cream, mustard, Worcestershire sauce, hot sauce and nutmeg; cook gently, whisking, until thickened and smooth. Reduce heat to low and gently simmer, stirring often, for 5 minutes. Stir in Velveeta, and 1 1/2 cups (375 mL) each of the Gruyère and Cheddar and 1 cup (250 mL) of the Parmesan; cook, stirring, until cheese is melted and sauce is smooth.

Fold reserved macaroni noodles into sauce; transfer to large baking dish. In bowl, stir together reserved Gruyère, Cheddar and Parmesan, butter, bread crumbs and crushed crackers; evenly spread over macaroni mixture. Bake in 350°F (180°C) oven until bubbling and golden brown, about 50 minutes.

Makes 6 servings, with leftovers

SUNDAY PRIME RIB ROAST

with SIMPLE PAN GRAVY
AND SKILLET POTATO GRATIN

The Sunday roast remains a classic family treat for many Nova Scotians. Cuts include top sirloin, eye of round or even hip, but a slow-roasted prime rib is the favourite for many meat lovers. A few key points here: First, hold off on salting the beef until after it is cooked; salt draws out moisture, so this retains more juices in the roast. Second, if you choose the bone-in cut, ask your butcher to remove the chine bone with his bandsaw, to make carving easier. Third, buy an internal-read thermometer and check the roast periodically; this is the best way to determine doneness. Finally, there is an ongoing debate about whether to start on a high heat, then reduce the temperature to obtain a nice crust on the outside, or whether to pan-sear the outside, then simply roast slowly on a low temperature. For me, not searing and simply roasting slowly produces a lovely colour, is easier and tidier, and ensures a juicy result. The only problem with this is that the roast retains so much juice there is not much juice caramelized on the bottom of the pan. So, using some beef stock is essential for making the pan gravy.

ROAST
INGREDIENTS

1 AA or AAA boneless or bone-in prime rib roast

2 onions, thinly sliced

2 carrots, sliced

1 stalk celery, chopped

2 sprigs fresh rosemary

8 sprigs fresh thyme

3 bay leaves

¼ cup (60 mL) extra-virgin olive oil

2 bulbs garlic, unpeeled and tops trimmed

1 tsp (5 mL) pepper

3 cups (750 mL) best-quality beef stock

2 tsp (10 mL) Worcestershire sauce

Salt and pepper to taste

Skillet Potato Gratin (recipe follows)

METHOD

Remove roast from refrigerator; let stand for 1 hour at room temperature. Preheat oven to 230°F (110°C). Position one rack in lowest slot. Thoroughly wash second rack and slide into next slot up. In wide shallow roasting pan, arrange onions, carrots, celery, rosemary, thyme and bay leaves; Drizzle 2 tbsp (30 mL) of the oil overtop and toss to coat. Place garlic, cut-side down, in pan. Place pan on lower rack in oven.

Pat roast dry with paper towel; rub all over with remaining oil and sprinkle with pepper. Transfer directly onto upper rack in oven; cook until desired doneness, 3 to 6 hours (do not open door for first 2 hours, then begin checking internal-read thermometer every 30 minutes). When the internal-read thermometer registers 125° to 130°F (50° to 54°C), your roast is medium-rare. Remove pan from the oven. Transfer roast from oven to rack; tent with foil and let stand for up to 90 minutes.

SIMPLE PAN GRAVY

Remove garlic from pan; discarding skin, carefully squeeze out cloves into the pan. Place over high heat on 2 burners; cook vegetables until sizzling. Stir in beef stock and cook, scraping off any brown bits from bottom and sides of pan with wooden spoon. When pan is "clean," mash together vegetables and stock; bring to a boil and cook for 2 minutes. Transfer to colander and strain into saucepan, using ladle to press moisture from solids. Discard solids. Stir in Worcestershire sauce and salt and pepper. Keep the sauce on a very low heat until ready to serve.

To really "beef up" the meal, you could choose many side dishes — from mashed potatoes to Yorkshire pudding. Scalloped potatoes are a local favourite, but I've never liked the usually bland and milky casserole with sliced raw onions. This richer and more exciting version resembles pomme dauphinoise — the cheese and fried onions make all the difference.

SKILLET POTATO GRATIN
INGREDIENTS

¼ cup (60 mL) butter

1 lb (500 g) onions, sliced

3 cloves garlic, minced

Salt and pepper to taste

Butter or olive oil, for greasing

2 lb (1 kg) Yukon Gold potatoes, scrubbed and unpeeled

1 ½ cups (325 mL) heavy cream (35% mf)

1 cup (250 mL) shredded Gruyère cheese

1 cup (250 mL) grated aged white Cheddar

½ cup (125 mL) grated Parmesan cheese

2 tbsp (30 mL) fresh thyme

METHOD

In small skillet over medium-high heat, melt butter; sauté onions, garlic, salt and pepper until onions are golden and liquid has evaporated. Reduce heat to medium and sauté until deep golden, about 15 minutes. Transfer to bowl; set aside.

With mandoline, shave potatoes into ⅛-inch (3 mm) slices. With butter, grease large cast-iron skillet. Pour about one-fifth of the cream into skillet; arrange one-quarter of the potato slices, slightly overlapping in bottom of skillet; top with one-quarter of the onion mixture, and one-quarter each of the Gruyère, Cheddar, Parmesan and thyme. Repeat three times more, then pour remaining cream overtop. Cover with foil and bake in 350°F (180°C) oven until golden brown, about 45 minutes. Remove foil; bake for 30 minutes. Transfer to rack; let stand for 30 minutes before serving.

Makes 8 to 10 servings

MENU

HARVEST BRUSCHETTA

*roast field tomatoes
and basil with aged
Gouda*

. . .

*creamed chanterelles
with sage*

. . .

*grilled pear with blue
cheese and
cider vinegar honey*

HARVEST BRUSCHETTA

WITH ROAST FIELD TOMATOES AND BASIL WITH AGED GOUDA, CREAMED CHANTERELLES WITH SAGE *and* GRILLED PEAR WITH BLUE CHEESE AND CIDER VINEGAR HONEY

Almost any pub or casual restaurant in Nova Scotia lists bruschetta on the menu. Sadly, it often arrives as soggy garlic bread covered in chopped tomatoes, red onion and mozzarella cheese. When it's made properly, bruschetta is not only delicious but also full of possibilities, especially with summer-fresh vegetables. This trio of favourite variations respects the easy Italian tradition of toasting bread and topping it with foods at their peak of freshness.

HARVEST BRUSCHETTA
INGREDIENTS

1 loaf crusty French, sourdough or rustique bread
Extra-virgin olive oil
Salt and pepper to taste

METHOD

Preheat grill to medium-high. Cut bread into ¹/₂- to ³/₄-inch (1 to 2 cm) slices; brush both sides of each slice with oil and transfer to grill. Toast, turning occasionally, until grilled and almost blackened in spots; transfer Harvest Bruschetta to rack, sprinkle with salt and pepper and let cool. Use as base for Roast Field Tomato and Basil with Aged Gouda, Creamed Chanterelles with Sage, and Grilled Pear with Blue Cheese and Cider Vinegar Honey.

ROAST FIELD TOMATOES AND BASIL WITH AGED GOUDA
INGREDIENTS

2 large field tomatoes, stem ends removed and
    sliced ¹/₂-inch (1 cm) thick
1 tsp (5 mL) granulated sugar
1 tsp (5 mL) basil
¹/₂ tsp (2 mL) salt
¹/₂ tsp (2 mL) pepper
2 tbsp (30 mL) extra-virgin olive oil
1 clove garlic
¹/₂ cup (125 mL) fresh basil leaves
2 tbsp (30 mL) balsamic vinegar
2 oz (60 g) aged Gouda cheese, shaved in fine curls

METHOD

Arrange single layer of tomatoes on parchment paper–lined, rimmed baking sheet. In small bowl, stir together sugar, basil, salt and pepper; evenly sprinkle over tomatoes and drizzle with oil. Bake in 450°F (220°C) oven until edges are slightly charred, about 10 minutes.

   With spatula, gently transfer to plate. Pour juice from baking sheet into large glass measure; set aside.

   Rub garlic over Harvest Bruschetta. Top each with 2 or 3 basil leaves, then 2 slices tomato. Place 2 or 3 basil leaves overtop and drizzle with vinegar. Garnish with aged Gouda curls and a drizzle of reserved juice.

Makes 4 large bruschetta

CREAMED CHANTERELLES WITH SAGE
INGREDIENTS

8 oz (250 g) fresh chanterelle mushrooms

3 tbsp (45 mL) butter

1 shallot, finely chopped

1 clove garlic, finely chopped

¼ tsp (1 mL) salt

Pepper to taste

2 tbsp (30 mL) white wine

½ cup (125 mL) heavy cream (35% mf)

2 tbsp (30 mL) chopped parsley

1 tbsp (15 mL) chopped fresh sage

METHOD

Leave small chanterelles whole; tear or shred large ones so mushroom pieces are roughly same size and cook evenly.

In small saucepan over high heat, melt butter; sauté shallot until translucent, about 1 minute. Stir in chanterelles; cook for 1 minute. Stir in garlic, salt and pepper; sauté for 1 minute. Add wine; cook until wine has evaporated. Stir in cream, parsley and sage; cook until cream has reduced by half. Serve over warmed Harvest Bruschetta.

Makes 4 large bruschetta

You can clean chanterelle mushrooms by gently rubbing them with a dry tea towel or by using a mushroom brush, taking care to remove any bits of the "forest floor" from the underside. The difficulty of the cleaning job will depend on when they were picked: easy if the weather had been dry or more labour intensive if the weather had been damp. But as long as you don't use additional water during the cleaning, the chanterelles will taste spectacular and sauté nicely in the pan.

GRILLED PEAR WITH BLUE CHEESE AND CIDER VINEGAR HONEY
INGREDIENTS

¼ cup (60 mL) liquid honey

¼ cup (60 mL) apple cider vinegar

Pinch cayenne pepper

1 tbsp (15 mL) extra-virgin olive oil

1 tsp (5 mL) chopped fresh rosemary

Pinch salt and pepper

2 ripe Bosc pears

4 oz (125 g) blue cheese, crumbled

2 tbsp (30 mL) chopped fresh chives

METHOD

In small saucepan, stir together honey, vinegar and cayenne pepper; bring to a boil and cook until reduced by exactly half (only ¼ cup/60 mL remains). Remove from heat; set aside.

Preheat grill to high, ensuring rack is clean. In bowl, stir together oil, rosemary, salt and pepper. Slice pears into ½- to ¾-inch (1 to 2 cm) rounds, working from base to tip and leaving core in slices; toss in oil mixture to coat. Transfer to rack; grill until marked and slightly caramelized, 1½ to 2 minutes per side.

With tongs, transfer 3 or 4 slices to each Harvest Bruschetta and top with blue cheese; with tongs, transfer to rack, cover and grill until warmed through and cheese is slightly melted, 30 to 45 seconds. Transfer to serving platter; drizzle with reserved honey mixture and garnish with chives.

Makes 4 large bruschetta

PEAR
GINGERBREAD
CAKE
with DULCE DE LECHE AND CHANTILLY CREAM

This twist on the classic French tarte Tatin is made with my spicy Nova Scotia gingerbread cake recipe – first published in Anita Stewart's Canada in 2006. Anita claims it's her favourite warm gingerbread recipe of all time, and I am exceedingly proud of that compliment from such a culinary legend. Pears and ginger make a perfect couple – luckily.

Annapolis Valley Bosc or Bartlett pears are close to hand. Recently – like the rest of the world – I've fallen in love with dulce de leche, particularly when it's made with simple sweetened condensed milk cooked in a water bath. Delicious and decadent beyond words.

PEAR GINGERBREAD CAKE
INGREDIENTS

4 ripe pears
3/4 cup (175 mL) butter
1/4 cup (60 mL) granulated sugar
1/2 cup (125 mL) packed brown sugar
1 tbsp (15 mL) grated gingerroot
2 eggs
1 cup (250 mL) molasses
2 cups (500 mL) all-purpose flour
2 tsp (10 mL) baking powder
2 tsp (10 mL) cinnamon
1 tsp (5 mL) ground ginger
1/2 tsp (3 mL) ground cloves
1 tsp (5 mL) baking soda
1/2 tsp (2 mL) salt
1 cup (250 mL) boiling water
Dulce de Leche (recipe follows)
Chantilly Cream (recipe follows)

METHOD

With apple corer or melon baller, remove and discard cores from pears; slice widthwise into 1/8-inch (3 mm) rounds. In 10-inch (25 cm) cast-iron skillet over medium-high heat, stir together 1/4 cup (60 mL) of the butter and sugar until butter has melted and sugar is incorporated. Arrange pears in concentric circles on bottom of pan, using smaller slices to fill any gaps; cook, without disturbing slices, for 5 to 7 minutes.

In bowl, beat together remaining butter, brown sugar and gingerroot until light and fluffy. One at a time, add eggs, beating until incorporated; beat in molasses until smooth and blended.

In second bowl, sift together flour, baking powder, cinnamon, ginger, cloves, baking soda and salt. Gently beat flour mixture into butter mixture until stiff batter forms; beat in water until smooth, fluid batter forms. Pour over pears in pan. Bake in 350°F (180°C) oven until cake tester inserted in centre comes out clean, about 45 minutes. Let cool in pan on rack for about 30 minutes. Run knife along sides of pan to release cake; top pan with plate, invert plate and pan together, and lift off pan. Serve with Dulce de Leche and Chantilly Cream.

Makes 12 servings

DULCE DE LECHE
INGREDIENTS

Two 14-oz cans (396 g) sweetened condensed milk, unopened and
  labels removed
Pinch coarse sea salt

METHOD

Place steaming rack in large pot, set cans of milk on top and add
enough water to immerse cans. Cover and bring to a simmer; cook,
adding hot water occasionally to keep cans immersed, for 2 hours.
Remove from heat; let cool enough to handle. Open cans and scoop
thickened, caramelized milk into bowl; add salt and whisk until smooth.
Cover and refrigerate until ready to use. Before serving, rewarm in
saucepan or microwave.

Makes 1 ¾ cups (430 mL)

CHANTILLY CREAM
INGREDIENTS

2 cups (500 mL) heavy cream (35% mf)
2 tbsp (30 mL) icing sugar
1 tsp (5 mL) vanilla extract

METHOD

In bowl, beat or whisk together cream, icing sugar and vanilla until in
soft peaks.

Makes 3 cups (750 mL)

PUMPKIN
MOUSSE TORTE
WITH GINGERSNAP CRUST, SPICED PUMPKIN PRALINE, ORANGE CRANBERRY JAM SAUCE AND CHANTILLY CREAM

This popular dessert is the perfect balance between a traditional pumpkin pie and a more elegant cheesecake. Topped with a couple of fancy garnishes, it's quite light but full of flavour and not too sweet. It remains one of my favourite fall desserts, and each year, I look forward to

making it once I see the fields of the Annapolis Valley glow with spheres of burnt orange pumpkins. If the praline feels like too much work, just try some toasted pumpkin seeds and a drizzle of maple syrup instead.

PUMPKIN MOUSSE TORTE INGREDIENTS

One 8 oz (250 g) package gingersnap cookies
1/2 cup (125 mL) toasted pecans
1/4 cup (60 mL) melted butter
2 tbsp (30 mL) packed brown sugar
1 tsp (5 mL) cinnamon
1 package (8 oz/250 g) cream cheese, softened
1 cup (250 mL) icing sugar
4 gelatin leaves
1 1/4 cups (300 mL) heavy cream (35% mf), plus 2 tbsp (30 mL)
1 cup (250 mL) unsweetened pumpkin purée
1 tsp (5 mL) maple extract
1 tsp (5 mL) ground ginger
1 tsp (5 mL) cinnamon
1/2 tsp (2 mL) nutmeg
1/4 tsp (1 mL) ground cloves
Pinch salt
Spiced Pumpkin Praline (recipe follows)
Orange Cranberry Jam Sauce (recipe follows)
Chantilly Cream (recipe page 95)

METHOD

In food processor, pulse cookies until texture resembles fine meal; transfer to glass measure. In food processor, pulse pecans until texture resembles fine meal; return cookies along with butter, brown sugar and cinnamon; pulse until texture resembles moist crumble topping. Evenly press into bottom of 10-inch (25 cm) nonstick springform pan. Bake in centre of 350°F (180°C) oven until edges begin to colour, 10 to 12 minutes. Remove from heat and let cool completely in pan on rack.

In bowl, beat together cream cheese and icing sugar, scraping down sides, until light and fluffy, 4 to 5 minutes.

Place gelatin leaves in small bowl and just cover with cold water; let soak until softened, about 10 minutes. In saucepan, warm 2 tbsp (30 mL) heavy cream just until beginning to steam; with fingers, transfer gelatin leaves to pan and gently swirl pan until gelatin has dissolved. Set aside.

Beat together pumpkin purée, maple extract, ground ginger, cinnamon, nutmeg, cloves and salt into cream cheese mixture until blended and smooth. Beat in gelatin mixture until blended.

In second bowl, beat 1 1/4 cups (300 mL) cream until in stiff peaks. By thirds, gently fold into pumpkin mixture, maintaining as much air in cream as possible. With spatula, gently scrape into springform pan; gently level top. Cover and refrigerate for at least 12 hours before serving. Top each serving with Spiced Pumpkin Praline, Orange Cranberry Jam Sauce and Chantilly Cream.

Makes 10 to 12 servings

SPICED PUMPKIN PRALINE
INGREDIENTS

¾ cup (175 mL) shelled pumpkin seeds

1 tsp (5 mL) butter

½ tsp (2 mL) cinnamon

½ tsp (2 mL) ground allspice

½ tsp (2 mL) flaky sea salt

Pinch cayenne pepper

¾ cup (175 mL) granulated sugar

¼ cup (60 mL) water

1 tsp (5 mL) lemon juice

METHOD

In dry skillet over medium heat, gently toast pumpkin seeds, stirring occasionally, until fragrant and golden, about 5 minutes; remove from heat and let cool. With butter, grease nonstick rimmed baking sheet; transfer even layer of pumpkin seeds to pan.

In small bowl, stir together cinnamon, allspice, sea salt and cayenne pepper; set aside. In saucepan, bring sugar, water and lemon juice to a boil; cook, without swirling, until mixture begins to caramelize, 9 to 10 minutes (do not overcook; if hard sugar granules get stuck to pan side, brush down with water-moistened pastry brush). Carefully and evenly pour over pumpkin seeds to cover; while caramel coating is still soft and warm, sprinkle reserved cinnamon mixture over pumpkin seeds. Let cool until solid; with fingers, break into small shards and/or crumble.

Makes 1 cup (250 mL)

ORANGE CRANBERRY JAM SAUCE
INGREDIENTS

2 cups (500 mL) frozen cranberries

1 cup (50 mL) granulated sugar

1 cup (250 mL) cranberry juice

¼ cup (60 mL) Grand Marnier or Triple Sec liqueur

1 tsp (5 mL) vanilla extract

¼ tsp (1 mL) ground allspice

Zest and juice of 2 oranges

1 cup (250 mL) dried cranberries

METHOD

In saucepan, stir together frozen cranberries, sugar, cranberry juice, liqueur, vanilla, allspice, and orange zest and juice; bring to a boil. Reduce heat and simmer until cranberries begin to soften and fall apart, about 20 minutes. Transfer to blender and purée until smooth; through fine-mesh sieve and discarding solids, strain into bowl. Stir in dried cranberries; bring sauce back to a simmer and cook gently, stirring often, for 20 minutes. Transfer to airtight container and refrigerate until very cold.

Before serving, check consistency. To thin, stir in water or cranberry juice, 1 tbsp (15 mL) at a time.

Makes 2 ½ cups (675 mL)

Adjusting the sauce consistency can be done by adding some water or a little cranberry juice, a spoonful at a time, until you get a sauce that will hold the dried cranberries in suspension but still be less thick than a traditional cranberry sauce served with turkey at Christmas or Thanksgiving. The sauce should fall off a spoon slowly, not in one big clump.

East Coast Reuben Sandwich with
*Boiled Salt Beef, Sauerkraut, Swiss Cheese and
Thousand Island Dressing*

page 110

MARITIME TEA: OATCAKES, SHORTBREADS AND RAISIN BUTTER TARTS

"KALE, CAESAR!" SALAD

ROASTED ROOT VEGETABLES AND HAM HOCK SOUP

SWEET POTATO SOUP WITH MUSSEL AND CHORIZO RAGOUT, CILANTRO
PESTO AND LIME CRÈME FRAÎCHE

EAST COAST REUBEN SANDWICH WITH BOILED SALT BEEF, SAUERKRAUT,
SWISS CHEESE AND THOUSAND ISLAND DRESSING

SALT COD FRITTERS WITH SMOKED RED PEPPER AND OLIVE OIL SAUCE

WINTER

CORRIE HOTPOT

TURKEY POT PIE WITH APPLE CRANBERRY CHUTNEY

GRILLED LUNENBURG SAUSAGES WITH BRAISED RED CABBAGE

LAMB SHANK SHEPHERD'S PIE WITH SMOKED GOUDA MASH, MINTED
GARDEN PEAS AND ROASTED CARROTS

CHRISTMAS PLUM PUDDING

WARM VANILLA RICE PUDDING WITH STEWED CHERRIES AND CHOCOLATE

MENU

MARITIME TEA

oatcakes

. . .

shortbreads

. . .

raisin butter tarts

MARITIME TEA

OATCAKES, SHORTBREADS
AND RAISIN BUTTER TARTS

{
I've collected the best of these classic family recipes for the traditional baked goods that Nova Scotians will serve when entertaining at tea time. They really are the best, and I'm proud to include them in this book.
}

MARY TOUESNARD'S OATCAKES

These Cape Breton oatcakes are light, thin and crisp. Simply authentic — none of that new-fangled dipping in chocolate or filling with peanut butter — these will rival anything in the finest tea houses of Scotland.

INGREDIENTS

3 cups (750 mL) all-purpose flour
3 cups (750 mL) large-flake rolled oats
1 cup (250 mL) granulated sugar
2 tsp (10 mL) salt
1 tsp (5 mL) baking soda
1 cup (250 mL) cold butter
1 cup (250 mL) shortening
1/4 cup (60 mL) boiling water
1 tsp (5 mL) vanilla extract

METHOD

In bowl, whisk together flour, oats, sugar, salt and baking soda; with 2 knives or pastry cutter, cut in butter and shortening until mixture resembles meal. Stir in water and vanilla; with hands, form dough into ball.

On lightly floured work surface, place dough and cover with plastic wrap; over wrap, roll out dough to 1/4-inch (5 mm) thickness. Remove plastic and lightly sprinkle dough with flour. Cut into 2 1/2-inch (6 cm) squares; transfer to nonstick or parchment paper–lined baking sheet. Bake in 375°F (190°C) oven until edges are slightly browned, 12 to 15 minutes.

Makes 36 oatcakes

NANNY'S CHRISTMAS SHORTBREADS

Here's another easy, almost-perfect recipe I inherited from my Halifax grandmother. She usually presented these with a simple dollop of pink icing or a tiny piece of candied cherry in the centre, but I like making these using a decorative, ceramic cookie press.

INGREDIENTS

1 cup (250 mL) butter
1/2 cup (125 mL) icing sugar
2 tsp (10 mL) vanilla extract
1 1/4 cups (300 mL) all-purpose flour
1/2 cup (125 mL) cornstarch

METHOD

In bowl, cream together butter and icing sugar until light and smooth. Stir in vanilla. Stir in flour and cornstarch until dough forms. Transfer to lightly floured work surface; knead just until dough forms smooth ball with few visible cracks. With fingers, pull off small handfuls and form into 1 1/2-inch (3.5 cm) balls; transfer to baking sheet. Press each with decorative ceramic cookie press. Place on greased or parchment-lined baking tray. Bake in 325°F (160°C) oven just until edges are beginning to brown, 20 to 25 minutes. Let cool in pans on rack.

Makes 10 to 12 cookies

MY MOM'S RAISIN BUTTER TARTS

I can't even imagine a Christmas without my mother's butter tarts. I love them because they're delicious, but not sickly sweet, and the filling is nearly foolproof.

INGREDIENTS

2 ½ cups (625 mL) all-purpose flour
1 tbsp (15 mL) granulated sugar
1 tsp (5 mL) salt
²/₃ cup (150 mL) cold unsalted butter, cubed
¹/₃ cup (75 mL) cold vegetable shortening, cubed
½ cup (125 mL) ice water
2 eggs
1 ½ cups (375 mL) packed brown sugar
1 cup (250 mL) seedless raisins
½ cup (125 mL) melted butter
2 tbsp (30 mL) lemon juice
1 tsp (5 mL) cornstarch
1 tsp (5 mL) vanilla extract

METHOD

Sift flour, sugar and salt into large glass measure; transfer to food processor. Add cold butter and shortening and pulse until mixture resembles coarse bread crumbs. With food processor on high speed, pour in ice water; process until dough forms ball. On lightly floured work surface, knead 2 to 3 times; wrap in plastic wrap and refrigerate for at least 30 minutes.

Meanwhile, in bowl, with fork, stir together eggs, brown sugar, raisins, melted butter, lemon juice, cornstarch and vanilla.

On lightly floured surface, roll out reserved dough about ¹/₈-inch (3 mm) thick. With 4-inch (10 cm) round cutter (or rim of glass), cut out rounds; press each into cup in nonstick muffin pan. With fork, pierce dough on bottom of pan once or twice. Evenly divide filling among cups to within ¼ inch (6 mm) from rims. Bake in 350°F (180°C) oven for 20 minutes.

Makes twelve 3-inch (8 cm) tarts

"KALE, CAESAR!" SALAD

Walk through nearly any farmers' market after November and you'll see an abundance of kale on nearly every table. A fashionable green — mostly for its reputation as a "superfood" — it has always been welcome in my kitchen each winter, since it's often the only local fresh green I can

find. Marinating salad greens in either lemon juice or vinegar seems counterintuitive, since acid causes delicate leaves to wilt, but kale benefits. The acid tenderizes the leaves and is simpler than blanching them in boiling water.

CAESAR SALAD
INGREDIENTS

2 bunches of curly green kale
1 lemon, halved and seeded
1/4 French-style crusty baguette
1/4 cup (60 mL) butter
1 clove garlic, finely chopped
1/3 cup (75 mL) capers
8 strips bacon, cut in 1/2-inch (5 cm) lengths
1/4 cup (60 mL) water
1 cup (250 mL) canola or vegetable oil
Dressing (recipe follows)
1/2 cup (125 mL) grated Parmesan cheese
Pepper
Lemon wedges (optional)

METHOD

Remove and discard stems and tough outer leaves from kale; tear tender leaves into pieces roughly palm-size; rinse under cold running water and dry in spinner or pat dry with paper towel. Transfer to bowl; squeeze lemon overtop and gently rub the leaves together, massaging them in the lemon juice for about 30 seconds. Cover and refrigerate for at least 1 hour before use.

Tear baguette into irregular, crouton-size pieces. In large oven-proof skillet over medium-high heat, melt butter; gently sauté garlic for about 1 minute. Add baguette and sauté until coated with butter, about 2 minutes. Bake in 325°F (160°C) oven, tossing after 5 minutes, until crisp and golden, 7 to 10 minutes. Remove from heat; set aside.

Drain and thoroughly dry capers on paper towel. In small saucepan, heat oil to 350°F (180°C); sauté capers until floating and "blossomed," about 1 minute. With slotted spoon, transfer to paper towel to drain; let cool.

In skillet, bring bacon and water to a boil. Reduce heat to medium-high and cook until water has evaporated and bacon is crisp and browned; with slotted spoon, transfer to paper towel to drain. Keep warm until ready to use.

Drizzle reserved kale with about 1/4 cup (60 mL) of Dressing and add half the Parmesan; toss to thoroughly coat. Evenly arrange kale on large platter; sprinkle with reserved croutons, capers and bacon. Drizzle with about 1/4 cup (60 mL) of Dressing and sprinkle with remaining Parmesan and pepper. If desired, serve with lemon wedges on side.

Makes 6 to 8 lunch entrée salads

DRESSING
INGREDIENTS

4 cloves garlic

2 anchovy fillets

Zest and juice of 2 lemons

1 tbsp (15 mL) capers

1 tsp (5 mL) Worcestershire sauce

1 tsp (5 mL) Dijon mustard

1 tsp (5 mL) hot sauce

Pinch salt and pepper

3 egg yolks

1 cup (250 mL) canola oil

1/2 cup (125 mL) grated Parmesan cheese

METHOD

In blender, purée together garlic, anchovies, lemon zest and juice,
capers, Worcestershire sauce, mustard, hot sauce, salt and pepper
until smooth and blended. Add egg yolks and purée until incorporated.
With blender on medium speed, slowly pour in thin stream of oil
until emulsified; add Parmesan and pulse until smooth and blended.
Test, then adjust salt and pepper, if desired (dressing should be very
peppery with a strong lemon flavour). Transfer to airtight container and
refrigerate until ready to use.

Makes about 1 1/2 cups (325 mL)

ROASTED ROOT VEGETABLES *and* HAM HOCK SOUP

You could realistically call this soup "winter cellar veggie soup" as it features all those things we have plenty of all winter long in Nova Scotia. If you omit the ham hock and use only vegetable stock, you'll have a delicious vegetarian version. A dedicated meat eater, I do love the warm and satisfying meal that this soup provides — with all of the ingredients. You can garnish it with a drizzle of maple syrup, balsamic vinegar or melted butter, or with pieces of honey-roasted carrot. Paired with a piece of buttered bread or a biscuit, this is a classic stick-to-your-ribs winter treat.

INGREDIENTS

1 large (or 2 small) ham hock
4 cloves garlic
2 whole cloves
2 bay leaves
1 onion, halved
1 stalk celery
1 whole carrot
1 onion, coarsely chopped
2 cups (500 mL) diced sweet potatoes
2 cups (500 mL) diced turnips
2 cups (500 mL) diced parsnips
2 cups (500 mL) diced celery root
1 cup (250 mL) diced carrots
1/3 cup (75 mL) olive oil
1 tsp (5 mL) salt
1 tsp (5 mL) pepper
4 to 6 cups (1 to 1.5 L) chicken stock
4 cloves garlic, halved
1 tbsp (15 mL) summer savory, thyme or sage
1/2 cup (125 mL) heavy cream (35% mf) (optional)

METHOD

In stockpot, combine ham hock, 4 cloves garlic, cloves, bay leaves, halved onion, celery and whole carrot; cover with cold water and simmer until ham is falling off bone, about 2 hours. With tongs, transfer hock to plate and let cool. Through fine-mesh sieve and discarding solids, strain stock into bowl and set aside for soup.

Pick ham from bone; with fingers, finely shred. Transfer to bowl, moisten with a few drops of reserved ham stock, cover and refrigerate until ready to use. Discard bone.

In large bowl, toss together chopped onion, sweet potatoes, turnips, parsnips, celery root, carrots and oil; sprinkle with salt and pepper. Evenly spread on 2 rimmed baking sheets; bake in 400°F (200°C) oven until vegetables are beginning to caramelize, about 30 minutes. Transfer to clean stockpot; cover with reserved ham stock and top with 4 cloves garlic, halved, and summer savory. Add chicken stock to pot until liquid comes at least 1 inch (2.5 cm) above vegetables; bring to a boil. Reduce heat and simmer for 30 minutes; with immersion blender, purée to slightly coarse texture. Stir in ham. If desired for richer broth, stir in cream.

Makes 12 servings

SWEET POTATO SOUP

with MUSSEL AND CHORIZO RAGOUT
CILANTRO PESTO AND LIME CRÈME FRAÎCHE

Almost 20 years ago, when I apprenticed with Chef Michael Smith at The Inn at Bay Fortune, his signature dish was a sweet potato and mussel chowder — and it was awesome!

I developed my own variation of that unique dish, using cultivated mussels from Nova Scotia and an updated flavour base that's got heat from chorizo sausage and tangy citrus zip.

SWEET POTATO SOUP
INGREDIENTS

3 lb (1.5 kg) fresh mussels

$1/2$ cup (125 mL) water

6 cups (1.5 mL) diced sweet potatoes

3 tbsp (45 mL) extra-virgin olive oil

$1/4$ cup (60 mL) butter

2 cloves garlic, coarsely chopped

2 cups (500 mL) diced onions

1 cup (250 mL) diced celery

1 cup (250 mL) diced carrots

Salt and pepper to taste

2 pods star anise

2 sprigs fresh thyme

2 bay leaves

6 cups (1.5 L) vegetable stock

$1/2$ cup (125 mL) heavy cream (35% mf)

2 or 3 links fresh chorizo sausage

$1/2$ cup (125 mL) Cilantro Pesto (recipe follows)

Lime Crème Fraîche (recipe follows)

Sprigs of fresh cilantro

METHOD

Under cold running water, scrub and de-beard mussels, discarding any that are damaged or don't close when lightly tapped; transfer to large stockpot along with water. Cover and bring to a boil; cook until mussels have opened, about 4 minutes. Through sieve, strain cooking liquid into bowl; set aside. Discard any unopened mussels. Let mussels cool enough to handle. Pick meat from shells, discarding shells, and transfer to bowl; set aside.

In bowl, toss sweet potatoes with oil to coat; transfer to parchment paper–lined, rimmed baking sheet. Bake in 350°F (180°C) oven, stirring once halfway through, just until beginning to colour, about 20 minutes.

In stockpot over medium-high heat, melt butter; sauté garlic, onions, celery, carrots, salt and pepper just until onions are beginning to brown, about 10 minutes. Stir in sweet potatoes, star anise, thyme, bay leaves, vegetable stock and reserved mussel cooking liquid; bring to a boil. Reduce heat and simmer for about 1 hour. With tongs, remove and discard thyme sprigs and bay leaves (do not remove star anise). Transfer to blender with vented lid; purée. Through fine-mesh sieve and discarding solids, strain back into clean stockpot; stir in cream, salt and pepper and keep warm until ready to serve.

Cut sausage into single links; cut open 1 end of each. With fingers, pinch out meat in each casing, shaping irregular $1/2$-inch (1 cm) balls; discard casings. Transfer meat to large nonstick skillet over high heat; sauté, reducing heat slightly when fat is released, until cooked through and beginning to brown all over, 5 or 6 minutes. Reduce heat to low and stir in mussels; cook until warmed through; toss in Cilantro Pesto to coat.

Ladle about 1 $1/2$ cups (375 mL) soup into individual pasta or other wide shallow serving bowls; pile sausage mixture on centre. Garnish with drizzle of Lime Crème Fraîche and sprig of cilantro.

Makes 8 to 10 servings

CILANTRO PESTO
INGREDIENTS

1 bunch fresh cilantro, well rinsed and woody stems removed
½ cup (125 mL) toasted unsalted pistachio nuts
½ cup (125 mL) extra-virgin olive oil
2 tbsp (30 mL) grated gingerroot
Zest and juice of 2 limes
¼ cup (60 mL) grated Parmesan cheese (optional)
Pinch cayenne pepper
Pinch salt
Pepper

METHOD

Dry cilantro on paper towel or in salad spinner; set aside several sprigs for garnish.

In food processor on high, pulse together remaining cilantro, pistachios, oil, gingerroot and lime zest and juice until coarsely chopped; scrape down sides and purée until blended and smooth (to thin, add a little more oil). Add Parmesan, cayenne pepper, salt and pepper; pulse to blend. Transfer to airtight container and refrigerate until ready to use.

Makes 1 ½ cups (375 mL)

This recipe will yield a little more than what you need for the soup, so I use the remainder as a spread on paninis, a sauce for a Thai-inspired chicken pizza or even as a pasta sauce. If you don't see a use for it right away, it will keep for 6 months in the freezer.

LIME CRÈME FRAÎCHE
INGREDIENTS

1 cup (250 mL) heavy cream (35% mf)
2 tbsp (30 mL) buttermilk
Zest and juice of 1 lime

METHOD

In Mason jar, combine cream, buttermilk and lime zest and juice; attach lid and shake to mix. Let stand at room temperature until thickened to consistency of lightly whipped cream, at least 8 hours or up to 24 hours. Use immediately or refrigerate for up to 10 days.

Makes 1 cup (250 mL)

EAST COAST
REUBEN SANDWICH
WITH BOILED SALT BEEF, SAUERKRAUT,
SWISS CHEESE and THOUSAND ISLAND DRESSING

Salted beef brisket is a Nova Scotia classic, especially when it's the main ingredient of a Jiggs' dinner with cabbage, carrots, turnips and potatoes. This province is also famous for the sauerkraut made on Tancook Island for many, many years. But when I think of tender, braised salt beef and zippy homemade sauerkraut, a Reuben sandwich comes instantly to mind. The sauerkraut recipe here is very simple to prepare, but you can choose artisanal sauerkraut, instead. Rye bread is classic, but I've also made this with a wholesome Red Fife wheat or 12-grain bread, and it's equally flavourful. Serve with a crunchy dill pickle.

REUBEN SANDWICH
INGREDIENTS

3 lb (1.5 kg) salted beef brisket (corned beef)
10 whole peppercorns
2 whole cloves
2 bay leaves
1 onion, halved
1 carrot, cut in chunks
1 clove garlic
1 tsp (5 mL) summer savory
1/4 cup (60 mL) butter, softened
8 slices light rye bread
1/2 cup (125 mL) Thousand Island Dressing (recipe follows)
2 cups (500 mL) Sauerkraut (recipe follows)
1 lb (500 g) sliced Swiss cheese

METHOD

In large bowl, cover beef with cold water; let soak, changing water at least twice, for 12 to 24 hours. Transfer to stockpot and add just enough fresh cold water to cover. Around beef, arrange peppercorns, cloves, bay leaves, onion, carrot, garlic and savory; bring to a simmer and cook, topping up water if necessary, until beef is softened and fork-tender, about 2 hours. Remove from heat; let beef cool in stock in pot. With tongs, remove beef, discarding stock. With fingers, shred beef; remove and discard any fat or sinew.

Preheat large skillet or griddle over medium heat. Butter one side of each of 4 slices of bread and place, butter down, on countertop; spread each with about 1 tbsp (15 mL) Thousand Island Dressing, then top with about 1/2 cup (125 mL) of reserved beef. Spread with about 1 tbsp (15 mL) Sauerkraut; top with 2 slices Swiss cheese, then spread with another 1 tbsp (15 mL) Thousand Island Dressing. Butter one side of each remaining 4 slices of bread and place over each "open-face" sandwich, buttered side up. Transfer to skillet; reduce heat to medium and grill, turning once halfway through, until cheese has melted and bread is crisp and golden, about 4 to 5 minutes per side.

Makes 4 large sandwiches with beef left over

Do not rush the sandwich by turning up the heat – the key to every grilled cheese is "low and slow," so take your time. I usually cover the pan with a lid or an inverted mixing bowl, creating a stovetop oven that helps heat the sandwich through.

SAUERKRAUT
INGREDIENTS

1 head green cabbage
1 ½ tbsp (22 mL) coarse sea salt or kosher salt
1 tsp (5 mL) caraway seeds
1 tsp (5 mL) juniper berries
1 bay leaf

METHOD

Halve cabbage; remove and discard core. Julienne leaves into ⅛-inch (3 mm) strips; transfer to bowl. Sprinkle with salt, caraway seeds and juniper berries; with hands, massage cabbage, coating with seasoning, until cabbage is moist, wilting and beginning to release liquid, about 5 minutes. Transfer into 6-cup (1.5 L) Mason jar, firmly pressing into jar with end of clean wine bottle. Poke bay leaf down into centre; add any liquid from bowl.

Choose smaller jar that fits inside mouth of Mason jar; fill with water and push right down into Mason jar to press cabbage mixture as it ferments. Lay cheesecloth across top of Mason jar; screw band only (not lid) overtop or secure cheesecloth with elastic band. Let stand at room temperature for 24 hours, pressing cabbage mixture every few hours and skimming off any scum on surface. Check to ensure that cabbage has released enough liquid to fully immerse sauerkraut; if not, pour in enough salt water (1 tbsp/15 mL salt per 1 cup /250 mL water) to cover. Let stand at room temperature for 48 hours or up to 10 days (usually 5 days total fermentation is about right) before using.

Makes about 3 cups (750 mL)

Stored in an airtight container in the refrigerator, this sauerkraut keeps for up to 2 months. It is extremely versatile and can be used as a side or garnish to many dishes, including the Saturday Supper (page 130) and Lunenburg Sausages (page 118) recipes in this book, or simply on top of grilled sausages or hot dogs with some yellow mustard.

THOUSAND ISLAND DRESSING
INGREDIENTS

2 egg yolks
1 tbsp (15 mL) Dijon mustard
¼ tsp (1 mL) salt
¼ tsp (1 mL) pepper
1 cup (250 mL) vegetable oil, in glass measure
1 tbsp (15 mL) lemon juice
1 clove garlic, minced
¼ cup (60 mL) ketchup
¼ cup (60 mL) sweet green relish
2 tbsp (30 mL) finely chopped red onion
1 tbsp (15 mL) capers, finely chopped
1 tbsp (15 mL) red wine vinegar
1 tsp (5 mL) granulated sugar
½ tsp (1 mL) Tabasco sauce

METHOD

Sandwich damp towel between work surface and bottom of bowl. In bowl, whisk together egg yolks, mustard, salt and pepper until blended and smooth. Pour oil into egg mixture in slow, steady stream, whisking constantly, until thickened into mayonnaise, 2 to 3 minutes. Whisk in lemon juice to finish dressing base.

Gently whisk in garlic, ketchup, relish, onion, capers, vinegar, sugar and Tabasco sauce. If not using immediately, transfer to airtight container and refrigerate for up to 3 days until ready to use.

Makes about 2 cups (500 mL)

If you have chosen to use a pasteurized, store-bought mayonnaise for this recipe, the prepared dressing will last much longer in the fridge, up to 10 days.

SALT COD FRITTERS
WITH SMOKED RED PEPPER
and OLIVE OIL SAUCE

My family's heritage in Cape Breton is French-Basque. While the flavours from Spain and the Pyrenees mountains never made it onto our kitchen table when I was a child, salt cod certainly did. This little dish is inspired by the tapas bars of Barcelona, the pintxos bars of San Sebastián and the French dish of brandade. Whatever the flavour notes, these are Nova Scotia salt cod fish cakes at heart. The fun international twist makes them perfect for party finger foods or a fancy appetizer.

FRITTERS
INGREDIENTS

1 lb (500 g) salt cod fillets
2 large russet potatoes
2 cloves garlic, crushed
1 cup (250 mL) whole milk
¼ cup (60 mL) butter
1 tsp (5 mL) dry summer savory
¼ cup (60 mL) all-purpose flour
½ tsp (2 mL) paprika
¼ tsp (1 mL) pepper
2 eggs
1 egg yolk
¼ cup (60 mL) chopped Italian parsley
Canola oil
Smoked Red Pepper and Olive Oil Sauce (recipe follows)

METHOD

In large bowl, immerse cod in cold water; refrigerate, changing water 2 or 3 times per day, for 24 to 36 hours (if fillets are small, salt may leach out in about 8 hours; taste small piece of fillet about every 4 hours and adjust soaking time accordingly). In pot of boiling water, blanch cod for 8 minutes; with slotted spoon and reserving cooking liquid in pot, transfer to plate. Let cool; with fingers, break into flakes, removing and discarding any bones and skin. Set aside.

Peel potatoes and coarsely slice; transfer to pot with reserved cooking liquid. Bring to a boil and cook until fork-tender, about 10 minutes; drain and mash until smooth. Set aside.

In saucepan, stir together garlic, milk, butter and summer savory; bring to a simmer. Stir in flour, paprika and pepper; cook, stirring vigorously, until thickened to pasty sauce. Remove from heat; stir in reserved cod and potatoes until incorporated and slightly cooled. Stir in eggs, egg yolk and parsley until blended and smooth. Let stand for 15 minutes (if not ready to use, transfer to bowl, cover and refrigerate for up to 24 hours).

In heavy-bottomed, steep-sided pot, heat several cups oil until thermometer registers 350°F (180°C); with spoon, drop in batter about 1 tsp (5 mL) at a time (irregular shapes cook into crispier fritters); cook until bobbing on surface. With slotted spoon, transfer to paper towel to drain.

Serve as entrée accompanied by warmed Smoked Red Pepper and Olive Oil Sauce or, if serving as appetizers, ladle about ¼ cup (60 mL) Smoked Red Pepper and Olive Oil Sauce on individual small serving plates, then top with 4 or 5 fritters.

It is unlikely that the fritters will need salt, but taste one and adjust the seasonings if desired. I often sprinkle them with a small amount of paprika.

Makes approximately 24 fritters

SMOKED RED PEPPER AND OLIVE OIL SAUCE
INGREDIENTS

4 sweet red peppers
Small amount of olive oil
$^3/_4$ cup (175 mL) fine wood chips
2 cloves garlic, sliced
1 shallot, finely chopped
1 red chili pepper, seeded and finely chopped
1 tsp (5 mL) smoked paprika
1 tsp (5 mL) dry mustard
2 tbsp (30 mL) pure maple syrup
1 tbsp (15 mL) sherry vinegar
1 tbsp (15 mL) aged balsamic vinegar
$^1/_4$ tsp (1 mL) salt
$^1/_3$ cup (75 mL) extra-virgin olive oil

METHOD

Preheat broiler in oven to 500°F (260°C); slide top rack into second slot
down. Rub red peppers with small amount of oil and place on rimmed
baking sheet. Broil, turning often, until charred and blistered all over.
With tongs, transfer to bowl and cover with either a tea towel or
plastic wrap; let stand until cool enough to handle, about 30 minutes.
Remove and discard skins; break in half and remove and discard seeds
and cores.

Make stovetop smoker using a roasting pan with lid and a rack that
extends beyond rim of roasting pan. Set pan on burner. With foil, form
small tray with raised edges; evenly arrange wood chips on tray. Set
tray on bottom of pan directly above burner; set rack over pan. Arrange
peppers on rack; cover with lid. Smoke over high heat; when smoke
appears around lid, begin timing process. After 7 to 8 minutes, transfer
to cutting board; coarsely chop and set aside.

In saucepan over medium heat, warm about 1 tbsp (15 mL) of the oil;
sauté garlic, shallot and chili pepper for 1 to 2 minutes. Stir in paprika and
mustard; cook for 1 minute. Toss in reserved sweet peppers; transfer
to blender along with maple syrup, sherry vinegar, balsamic vinegar
and salt. Purée on high speed, scraping down sides once or twice, until
blended and smooth. Reduce speed and pour in remaining oil in smooth,
steady stream; purée until thickened and smooth. Transfer to small
saucepan; keep warm until ready to serve (do not let boil).

Makes about 1$^1/_2$ cups (375 mL)

CORRIE HOTPOT

Coronation Street has long been an enormously popular television show in Nova Scotia. Equally popular are the classic British comfort foods found on pub menus all over the province. This slow-baked casserole made famous on the show as Betty's (or Lancashire) hotpot is a dish few people would normally eat in this part of the world, but I want to introduce it into our culinary vernacular and give a respectful nod to our Commonwealth friends and fellow pub crawlers across the pond. Thanks for all the great Corrie years, meat pies, and fish and chips!

INGREDIENTS

2 lb (1 kg) lamb shoulder, cut in 1-inch (2.5 cm) cubes

2 tbsp (30 mL) all-purpose flour

3 tbsp (45 mL) vegetable oil

½ cup (125 mL) red wine

1 ½ cups (375 mL) diced carrots

1 ½ cups (375 mL) diced turnips

2 tbsp (30 mL) Worcestershire sauce

2 tbsp (30 mL) HP Sauce

2 tbsp (30 mL) ketchup

1 tbsp (15 mL) English mustard

1 tsp (5 mL) Tabasco sauce

1 tbsp (15 mL) chopped fresh rosemary

1 tsp (5 mL) summer savory

2 bay leaves

Salt and pepper to taste

2 cups (500 mL) thinly sliced onions

3 large Yukon Gold potatoes

2 tbsp (30 mL) butter, melted

Chopped parsley (optional)

METHOD

In large bowl, toss lamb with flour to coat all over. Heat large skillet over high heat until beginning to smoke; add oil. In two batches, brown lamb all over; with slotted spoon, transfer to second bowl. Add wine to pan and cook, stirring brown bits from bottom and sides of pan with wooden spoon, until reduced by half; pour over lamb.

Stir in carrots, turnips, Worcestershire sauce, HP sauce, ketchup, mustard, Tabasco sauce, rosemary and summer savory to thoroughly mix. Choose casserole dish with tight-fitting lid; evenly spread lamb mixture over bottom of dish. Top with bay leaves and sprinkle with salt and pepper; evenly cover with onions and sprinkle with salt and pepper.

With mandoline, thinly slice potatoes (do not rinse after slicing as starch helps to create tight seal); working from rim to centre, evenly overlap slices on lamb mixture in pinwheel pattern. Cover and place in preheated 350°F (180°C) oven; immediately reduce heat to 300°F (150°C) and bake, without removing lid, for 2 ½ hours. Remove from oven and increase temperature to 350°F (180°C). Uncover and brush potatoes with butter and sprinkle with salt and pepper. Return to oven and cook, uncovered, until golden, 30 to 45 minutes. Remove from oven and let stand for at least 1 hour before serving. If desired, garnish with parsley.

Makes 6 to 8 hearty servings

I use a classic Dutch oven with a tight-fitting lid for this recipe, but you can use any standard 4 quart (4 litre) deep casserole or earthenware dish as well. If you don't have one with a lid, simply use aluminium foil and create as tight a seal as you can, then weigh it down with a frying pan. The tight seal creates pressure and helps retain moisture and tenderizes the meat. Slicing the potatoes is made easier with a mandolin or Japanese vegetable slicer, but you can use a sharp knife as well. Just take your time and watch your fingertips!

TURKEY POT PIE
WITH APPLE CRANBERRY
CHUTNEY

This has become a bit of an "after Christmas dinner" tradition for my family and me, as it uses up a significant quantity of turkey leftovers on Boxing Day. However, you could take the same steps with cold chicken and obtain an equally delicious result anytime of the winter. For me, the key with meat pies is consistency, as I do not like extremely runny fillings. I prefer a bottom and a top crust, made in the style closer to a British meat pie. If you're rushed for time, you could assemble the filling and bake it in a casserole dish covered with just a top crust of pastry or sheet of store-bought all-butter puff pastry.

PIE FILLING
INGREDIENTS

¼ cup (60 mL) butter

1 onion, finely chopped

1 stalk celery, finely chopped

1 carrot, finely chopped

1 cup (250 mL) sliced button mushrooms

1 tsp (5 mL) summer savory

1 tsp (5 mL) poultry seasoning

Salt and pepper to taste

¼ cup (60 mL) plus 1 tbsp (15 mL) all-purpose flour

¼ cup (60 mL) white wine

1 cup (250 mL) turkey stock

1 cup (250 mL) turkey gravy

¼ cup (60 mL) heavy cream (35% mf)

½ cup (125 mL) frozen sweet peas

1 tbsp (15 mL) chopped fresh sage

5 to 6 cups (1.25 to 1.5 L) light and dark cooked turkey meat

No-Fail Pie Crust (recipe follows)

1 egg, beaten with few drops water

METHOD

In large skillet over medium-high heat, melt butter; sauté onion, celery, carrot, mushrooms, summer savory, poultry seasoning, salt and pepper until mushrooms are beginning to release liquid. Reduce heat to medium and cook until almost all liquid has evaporated and pan looks dry, 10 or 12 minutes. Stir in ¼ cup (60 mL) flour to form roux; cook, stirring constantly, for 3 minutes.

Stir in wine; cook until wine has evaporated, about 3 minutes. Stir in turkey stock, turkey gravy and heavy cream. Reduce heat and simmer until thickened almost to paste, about 20 minutes. Remove from heat; gently stir in peas, sage and turkey meat. Transfer to bowl, cover and refrigerate until cooled.

Halve reserved dough from No-Fail Pie Crust; with hands, form 2 same-size balls. On lightly floured surface, roll out each into 14- to 16-inch (35 to 40 cm) round. Place one round into greased and lightly floured 10-inch (25 cm) deep-dish pie pan; fill with turkey mixture. Brush rim with egg mixture; cover with second round of dough, crimping edges together around rim to seal. With pastry tip or apple corer, cut venting hole in centre; brush crust with remaining egg mixture. Bake in 350°F (180°C) oven until crust is deep golden brown, 45 to 60 minutes.

Makes 4 to 6 servings

NO-FAIL PIE CRUST
INGREDIENTS

2 ½ cups (625 mL) unbleached white flour

1 tsp (5 mL) baking powder

½ tsp (2 mL) sea salt

½ cup (125 mL) vegetable shortening

½ cup (125 mL) salted butter

1 egg yolk

¾ cup (175 mL) ice water

1 tsp (5 mL) white vinegar

METHOD

In large bowl, whisk together flour, baking powder and salt; with
2 knives or pastry cutter, cut in shortening and butter until mixture
resembles coarse meal. In bowl, stir together egg yolk, ice water and
vinegar. Stir into flour mixture; lightly knead just until dough forms
(do not overwork). Tightly wrap in plastic; refrigerate for at least 30
minutes.

APPLE CRANBERRY CHUTNEY
INGREDIENTS

2 star anise pods

1 cinnamon stick

1 large Honeycrisp apple, diced

3 cups (750 mL) fresh or frozen cranberries

1 cup (250 mL) dried cranberries

½ cup (125 mL) granulated sugar

½ cup (125 mL) packed brown sugar

½ cup (125 mL) apple or cranberry juice

¼ tsp (1 mL) ground cloves

METHOD

In saucepan over medium-high heat, stir together star anise, cinnamon
stick, apple, fresh or frozen and dried cranberries, sugar, brown sugar,
apple juice and cloves; bring to a simmer and cook until cranberries
are softened and breaking apart, about 5 minutes. Reduce heat to
low; simmer, stirring often to prevent sticking, until thickened to
consistency of strawberry jam, about 15 minutes. Remove from heat;
let cool. Remove and discard cinnamon stick and star anise pod, then
transfer to airtight container and refrigerate for up to 3 weeks (or ladle
hot sauce into hot sterilized canning jars, seal and process according
to manufacturer's instructions).

Makes 3 cups (750 mL)

GRILLED LUNENBURG
SAUSAGES
with BRAISED RED CABBAGE

Every fall, the German heritage is signalled by small Oktoberfest events in towns such as Tatamagouche and most certainly in Halifax. But Lunenburg County showcases German cuisine year-round. There are the famous Tancook Island sauerkrauts, Lunenburg puddings and Lunenburg sausage made by several small butchers up and down the South Shore. The pudding is a softer coil filled with pork-and-beef entrails and spices. The sausage is a link made in the style of Polish sausage or kielbasa. Although sauerkraut makes a more traditional side dish (see East Coast Reuben Sandwich, page 110), for this, I actually prefer to serve braised red cabbage in the delicious German version. Cooked with apples and bacon, and spiced with caraway seeds and juniper berries, it's slightly sweet and sour and is perfect with the smoky grilled sausages and tangy mustard glaze. Mashed potatoes and a hunk of bread or a warm pretzel is all you need to make your dining room into a boisterous beer garden!

SAUSAGES
INGREDIENTS

¹/₄ cup (60 mL) mustard

1 tbsp (15 mL) liquid honey

1 tbsp (15 mL) chopped parsley

Pinch each salt and pepper

3 lb (1.5 kg) fresh Lunenburg sausages

Braised Red Cabbage (recipe follows)

METHOD

Preheat grill to medium heat. In small bowl, stir together mustard, honey, parsley, salt and pepper; set aside.

With tongs (to avoid piercing casings), place sausages on grill; cook, turning often to prevent sausages from heating too quickly and splitting, for about 7 minutes for small link sausages and 10 minutes for large single coil. When outside darkens, reduce heat to medium-low; brush with reserved mustard mixture and cook, turning, until glazed all over, about 10 minutes. Remove from heat; keep warm and let stand for at least 15 minutes. Slice sausage into ¹/₂-inch (1 cm) rounds; fan over platter of Braised Red Cabbage.

Makes 6 to 8 servings

BRAISED RED CABBAGE
INGREDIENTS

1 large head red cabbage (about 3 lb/1.5 kg), cored and quartered

6 strips of smoked bacon, cut in ½-inch (1 cm) lengths

6 whole juniper berries

3 whole cloves

1 red or yellow onion, thinly sliced

1 tsp (5 ml) caraway seeds

1 tsp (5 mL) salt

1 tsp (5 mL) pepper

2 apples, unpeeled and diced

2 bay leaves

1 stick cinnamon

¾ cup (175 mL) apple cider

¾ cup (175 mL) red wine

½ cup (125 mL) packed brown sugar

½ cup (125 mL) cider vinegar

METHOD

Thinly slice cabbage quarters into ⅛-inch (3 mm) strips; set aside.

In shallow braising pan over medium heat, sauté bacon until browned and beginning to release fat. Stir in juniper berries, cloves, onion, caraway seeds, salt and pepper; cook just until onion begins to brown, about 10 minutes.

Stir in reserved cabbage along with apples, bay leaves, cinnamon stick, cider, wine, brown sugar and vinegar; increase heat to high and cook, stirring often, until cabbage is darkened and beginning to release liquid, about 5 minutes. Cover with lid or seal with foil; transfer to 300°F (150°C) oven and bake for 45 minutes. Remove from heat and check liquid in bottom of pan; cabbage should be moist but not swimming in liquid. If necessary, return pan to stove over medium heat and cook until liquid is reduced as desired. Remove bay leaves before serving.

LAMB SHANK SHEPHERD'S PIE

WITH SMOKED GOUDA MASH, MINTED GARDEN PEAS *and* ROASTED CARROTS

I served a version of this dish at the James Beard House in 2008, to New York City epicureans as a representation of the flavours of Nova Scotia's North Shore. I wanted to show how a simple shepherd's pie could be elegant and deliver the taste of the season. A beloved meat in our world, lamb can be expensive at times, but there are flavourful ways to use cheaper cuts, and a shepherd's pie is a great way to feed a large group with a rich and satisfying meal. If you don't have lamb shanks, you could use a shoulder cut and the same method.

SHEPHERD'S PIE INGREDIENTS

6 lamb shanks (each about 12 oz/375 g)

½ cup (125 mL) vegetable oil

2 onions, coarsely chopped

2 stalks celery, coarsely chopped

2 carrots, coarsely chopped

¾ cup (175 mL) all-purpose flour

2 cups (500 mL) red wine or sherry

2 tbsp (30 mL) tomato paste

4 cups (1 L) lamb or beef stock

6 sprigs fresh thyme

4 sprigs fresh mint

4 bay leaves

Salt and pepper to taste

Smoked Gouda Mash (recipe follows)

Butter

Minted Garden Peas and Roasted Carrots (recipe follows)

METHOD

In Dutch oven over high heat, brown the lamb shanks all over in vegetable oil. Transfer to plate and set aside. In same pan, sauté onions, celery and carrots until slightly caramelized, about 10 minutes. Stir in flour; cook, stirring, for 1 or 2 minutes. Stir in wine and tomato paste; cook, stirring often and scraping up any brown bits from bottom and sides of pan, for 2 minutes. Stir in stock and bring to a boil; add in reserved shanks, thyme, mint and bay leaves (liquid should completely cover shanks); return to a boil.

Cover and transfer to 300°F (150°C) oven; braise for 2 ½ to 3 hours. Remove from oven; let stand in braising liquid for at least 2 hours, but preferably overnight in the refrigerator. With slotted spoon, transfer shanks to tray.

Through fine-meshed sieve or colander, strain braising liquid into saucepan over medium-high heat, discarding solids; cook until reduced into rich, gravy-like sauce thick enough to coat back of a spoon. Stir in salt and pepper. Remove from heat; set aside.

Pick meat from reserved shank bones; discard bones. Arrange meat on bottom of large baking dish; pour in 2 cups (500 mL) or enough reserved sauce to cover meat. With spatula, evenly spread Smoked Gouda Mash overtop and dot with butter; sprinkle with additional grated Gouda. Bake in 350°F (180°C) oven until top is crisp and browned, about 45 minutes. Serve with Minted Garden Peas and Roasted Carrots.

Makes 8 servings

SMOKED GOUDA MASH
INGREDIENTS

2 lb (1 kg) Yukon Gold potatoes, halved

½ cup (125 mL) butter

1 tsp (5 mL) salt

1 tsp (5 mL) pepper

2 cups (500 mL) shredded smoked Gouda cheese (plus extra ½ cup
for garnish)

2 eggs

METHOD

In large pot of boiling salted water, cook potatoes until fork-tender;
drain, then return potatoes to pan. Mash in butter, salt and pepper until
smooth; beat in Gouda and whole eggs until thoroughly mixed.

MINTED GARDEN PEAS AND ROASTED CARROTS
INGREDIENTS

2 tbsp (30 mL) liquid honey

1 tbsp (15 mL) extra-virgin olive oil

1 lb (500 grams) rainbow carrots, peeled and halved

Salt and pepper to taste

1 cup (250 mL) fresh peas

2 tbsp (30 mL) butter

1 tsp (5 mL) chopped fresh mint

1 tbsp (15 mL) water

METHOD

In bowl, stir together honey and oil; toss in carrots to coat. Transfer to
baking dish; roast in 400°F (200°C) oven until slightly caramelized,
20 to 25 minutes. Sprinkle with salt and pepper.

In small saucepan of boiling salted water, cook peas until tender but
slightly firm, about 3 minutes; drain. Transfer to small saucepan along
with butter, mint and water; cover and cook until liquid has evaporated
and peas are glazed. Sprinkle with salt and pepper.

CHRISTMAS PLUM PUDDING

I began making Christmas plum pudding – my father's favourite dessert of the entire year – after returning home from my apprenticeship in England, where it is the single-most-important ritual at the holiday table. Thinking I should be able to make a killer "pud," I took up the torch to relieve my mother of that particular annual duty. Every year thereafter, for about a decade, I played with a recipe I'd found in an old English traditions book. In 2014, I think I finally nailed it. This is the new standard plum pudding in

my repertoire, and I doubt it will change much from now on. It's very moist and spicy and is made with eggs, dairy and, yes, beef suet. It also uses a technique from sticky-toffee pudding recipes – that of puréeing boiled dates – which lends a lovely butterscotch-like flavour. The ingredient list is long but everything is easily found in any grocery store. Serve the pudding with the classic rum hard sauce, whipped cream, vanilla ice cream or Brown Sugar Brandy Sauce (page 155).

INGREDIENTS

12 pitted dates
¹/₂ cup (125 mL) water
4 eggs
¹/₂ cup (125 mL) heavy cream (35% mf)
¹/₂ cup (125 mL) buttermilk
¹/₂ cup (125 mL) treacle or molasses
¹/₄ cup (60 mL) unsalted butter, melted, plus extra for greasing (optional)
Dry Mixture (recipe follows)
Fruit Mixture (recipe follows)
¹/₄ lb (125 g) beef suet
1 apple, unpeeled and grated
¹/₄ cup (60 mL) warm brandy or rum (optional)

METHOD

In saucepan, combine dates and water; bring to a boil. Reduce heat and simmer until only about 1 tbsp (15 mL) water remains. Transfer to food processor and purée until smooth (if desired, transfer to airtight container and refrigerate until ready to use). Set aside.

In large bowl, beat together date purée, eggs, cream, buttermilk, treacle and butter.

Transfer Dry Mixture to second large bowl. In third large bowl, toss together Fruit Mixture, suet and apple; toss into Dry Mixture until thoroughly mixed. With wooden spoon, stir in reserved date mixture until moist doughy batter forms; cover and refrigerate for at least 2 hours.

Prepare 2 large heatproof ceramic bowls (or several smaller ramekins) by greasing with butter or food-release spray; line each with plastic wrap, leaving generous excess hanging over sides. With spatula, scrape pudding batter into bowls, leveling tops, then fold plastic wrap overtop to completely cover batter. Wrap foil over each bowl; secure just under rim of each with kitchen twine.

Set bowls in large baking dish or roasting pan; to dish, add enough water to come halfway up sides of bowls. Bake in 300°F (150°C) oven until cake tester inserted in centre comes out clean and centre is firm, 45 to 90 minutes (my 1 lb/500 g pudding bakes in about 90 minutes). Remove dish from oven; remove bowls from dish and transfer to rack. Let cool completely; invert each bowl to turn out wrapped pudding.

Just before serving, unwrap pudding. To serve traditionally, pour hot brandy or rum overtop, then use long wooden match to light a beautiful blue blaze, or simply reheat in a microwave for 30 seconds per individual portion.

Makes 12 to 14 servings

 You can test the puddings by tapping the centres with your finger, looking for firmness, or you can use a cake tester or bamboo skewer to see if the batter is set in the middle. Simply insert the skewer and see if it comes out clean with no wet batter clinging too it.

DRY MIXTURE

2 cups (500 mL) buttermilk-biscuit crumbs
1 ¼ cups (300 mL) all-purpose flour
1 cup (250 mL) packed brown sugar
2 tsp (10 mL) ground allspice
2 tsp (10 mL) ground ginger
2 tsp (10 mL) cinnamon
2 tsp (10 mL) grated gingerroot
1 tsp (5 mL) ground cloves
1 tsp (5 mL) nutmeg
¼ tsp (1 mL) salt

METHOD

In large bowl, whisk together biscuit crumbs, flour, brown sugar, allspice, ginger, cinnamon, gingerroot, cloves, nutmeg and salt. Use immediately or store in airtight container at room temperature until ready to use.

FRUIT MIXTURE
INGREDIENTS

1 cup (250 mL) chopped candied fruit, such as pineapple, red and
   green cherries
¼ cup (60 mL) golden raisins
½ cup (125 mL) seedless raisins
½ cup (125 mL) currants
½ cup (125 mL) finely chopped black Mission figs
½ cup (125 mL) candied peel
½ cup (125 mL) mixed dried fruit, such as pears, apples, peaches
½ cup (125 mL) finely chopped prunes
½ cup (125 mL) dried cranberries
½ cup (125 mL) finely chopped dried apricots
¼ cup (60 mL) brandy or rum
¼ cup (60 mL) port
2 tsp (10 mL) vanilla extract

METHOD

In large bowl, toss together candied fruit, golden raisins, seedless raisins, currants, figs, candied peel, dried fruit, prunes, cranberries and apricots. In small bowl or glass measure, stir together brandy, port and vanilla; toss into candied fruit mixture to coat. Transfer to airtight container; let stand at room temperature for at least 12 hours.

WARM VANILLA RICE PUDDING

with STEWED CHERRIES
AND CHOCOLATE

Risotto remains enormously popular in the Nova Scotia restaurant world, but few people have ever tried this rich and satisfying rice as a sweet dessert. I know it seem s odd, but in reality, this is just a warm rice pudding, something that is really quite familiar and comforting on a winter's night. In the base of the risotto, I use internationally renowned Nova Scotia ice wine. I have always been a fan of Black Forest cake, and this uses the wonderful Annapolis Valley sour cherries we have available here year-round, either in frozen or preserved form. To bring it all together, shavings of dark chocolate on top. A rice pudding like none other!

INGREDIENTS

3 cups (750 mL) whole milk

¼ cup (60 mL) butter

2 vanilla pods, halved lengthwise, seeds removed and reserved

¾ cup (175 mL) carnaroli or superfine arborio rice

¼ cup (60 mL) Nova Scotia ice wine

3 tbsp (45 mL) granulated sugar

¼ tsp (1 mL) cinnamon

⅛ tsp (0.5 mL) nutmeg

¼ cup (60 mL) heavy cream (35% mf)

Pinch salt

2 cups (500 mL) frozen or preserved cherries

¼ cup (60 mL) granulated sugar

Zest and juice of 1 orange

¼ cup (60 mL) kirsch or cherry liqueur

Fresh cherries

3 oz (90 g) bittersweet dark chocolate

Fresh mint leaves

METHOD

In saucepan, heat milk until almost simmering.

In steep-sided saucepan, melt 3 tbsp (45 mL) of the butter; stir in vanilla pods and reserved vanilla seeds. Stir in rice; sauté until coated and slightly shiny, about 3 minutes. Add wine and cook, stirring up any brown bits on bottom and sides of pan, until wine has been absorbed. Stir in sugar, cinnamon and nutmeg. Reduce heat to medium; one ladle at a time, add milk to rice mixture and cook, stirring with wooden spoon, until incorporated, 15 to 18 minutes. Stir in cream and salt; cook for 1 minute. Remove from heat; stir in remaining butter. With slotted spoon, remove and discard vanilla pods. Let risotto stand for 3 to 5 minutes before serving.

Meanwhile, in saucepan, stir together cherries, sugar and orange zest and juice (if using preserved cherries, you may skip adding orange juice here; preserved cherries will release their own liquid); bring to a rapid boil. Add kirsch; using a wooden match, carefully flambé cherry mixture. When flames burn out, remove from heat (do not allow syrup to reduce too much).

Ladle warm risotto into individual small serving plates or shallow soup bowls. Top with fresh cherries and drizzle with syrup. With box or microplane grater, shave several curls of chocolate over each; garnish with mint leaves.

Makes 6 to 8 servings

Smokehouse Sliders
with Smoked Gouda Cheese Slices; Scotch Barbecue
Sauce; Caramelized Onion, Bacon and Balsamic Jam;
Chipotle Mayo; and Crispy Fried Shallots

page 148

SATURDAY SUPPER WITH GRILLED SMOKED PORK CHOPS, BACON BAKED
BEANS AND MUSTARD PICKLES

BEST BREAKFAST SANDWICH WITH MAPLE AND APPLE SAUSAGE
WITH CHEDDAR AND ONION BISCUITS

FINNAN HADDIE

SEAFOOD CHOWDER

SNOW CRAB CAKES WITH GUACAMOLE

YEAR-ROUND

SMOKED SALMON PIZZA

THE HALIFAX DONAIR

CHICKEN DINNER POUTINE

THAI GREEN CHICKEN CURRY

SMOKEHOUSE SLIDERS WITH SMOKED GOUDA CHEESE SLICES; SCOTCH
BARBECUE SAUCE; CARAMELIZED ONION, BACON, AND BALSAMIC JAM;
CHIPOTLE MAYO AND CRISPY FRIED SHALLOTS

CHOCOLATE RUM CAKE WITH CHOCOLATE GANACHE AND
TOASTED-COCONUT ICE CREAM

CARROT PUDDING WITH BROWN-SUGAR BRANDY SAUCE

MENU

SATURDAY SUPPER

*grilled smoked
pork chops*

. . .

bacon baked beans

. . .

mustard pickles

SATURDAY SUPPER

with GRILLED SMOKED PORK CHOPS,
BACON BAKED BEANS AND MUSTARD PICKLES

Growing up, my Saturday supper was usually hot dogs with beans and mustard pickles, and maybe some Nova Scotia-made sauerkraut on the side. That combo's still a favourite, but I have come to prefer lovely Nova Scotia smoked pork chops purchased from one of our excellent local delis or butchers. I add some spiciness and throw them on the barbecue for extra flavour. Smoked pork chops are most often fully cooked and *simply need to be warmed through. It is also important to not overcook them as the flesh will dry out quickly. The side dishes are the very essence of a cold winter's supper, but this meal is satisfying in any season. Serve it with crusty rolls or sliced white country bread and butter. For me, this is possibly the greatest Nova Scotia-inspired supper in this book.*

GRILLED SMOKED PORK CHOPS
INGREDIENTS

1 tbsp (15 mL) olive or vegetable oil

1 tsp (5 mL) paprika

1 tsp (5 mL)) garlic powder

1 tsp (5 mL) pepper

1/8 tsp (0.5 mL) cayenne pepper

6 smoked bone-in pork chops, 1 1/4-inch (3 cm) thick

1 tsp (5 mL) salt

1 tbsp (15 mL) chopped parsley, for garnish

METHOD

Preheat grill to high. In small bowl, stir together oil, paprika, garlic powder, pepper and cayenne pepper; lightly brush all over chops. Grill 1 side of chops for 2 minutes; rotate each 90 degrees and grill for 2 minutes. Flip chops, and repeat to grill second sides.

Reduce heat to low, transfer chops to back of grill on highest rack and close lid; cook until chops are warm in centre, about 5 minutes. Remove from grill; let rest for 10 minutes before serving. Season with salt and sprinkle with parsley.

BACON BAKED BEANS
INGREDIENTS

1 cup (250 mL) double-smoked bacon, sliced in 1/4-inch (5 mm) lengths

1 onion, diced

1 tsp (5 mL) salt

1 tsp (5 mL) pepper

1 lb (500 g) dried navy beans, soaked overnight in water and drained

1/2 cup (125 mL) molasses

1/4 cup (60 mL) packed brown sugar

1/4 cup (60 mL) ketchup

1 tbsp (15 mL) Worcestershire sauce

2 tsp (10 mL) dry mustard

1 tsp (5 mL) hot sauce

1/2 tsp (2 mL) ground cloves

METHOD

In large skillet, sauté bacon until fat is released; stir in onion, salt and pepper and cook until onion is slightly browned, about 10 minutes. Stir in beans, molasses, brown sugar, ketchup. Worcestershire sauce, mustard, hot sauce and cloves; cover with enough water to come about 1/4-inch (5 mm) above mixture. Bring to a boil; remove from heat. Cover and bake in 300°F (150°C) oven, checking every 45 minutes and topping up water if necessary, until beans are fork-tender but slightly firm, about 2 1/2 hours.

MUSTARD PICKLES

INGREDIENTS

4 stalks celery, minced

10 cups (2.5 L) seeded diced unpeeled English cucumbers

5 cups (1.25 L) diced onions

1 cup (250 mL) minced sweet red pepper

1 cup (250 mL) minced sweet green pepper

½ cup (125 mL) rock salt

4 cups (1 L) boiling water

4 cups (1 L) white vinegar

4 cups (1 L) granulated sugar

3 tbsp (45 mL) yellow mustard seeds

3 tbsp (45 mL) dry mustard

3 tbsp (45 mL) turmeric

2 tbsp (30 mL) pepper

1 tbsp (15 mL) crushed fenugreek

1 tbsp (15 mL) ground cumin

½ cup (125 mL) cornstarch

METHOD

In large heatproof bowl, stir together celery, cucumbers, onions, red pepper and green pepper. Stir salt into boiling water until dissolved; pour over cucumber mixture, stirring vegetables to immerse; let stand for 2 hours. Drain and set aside.

In large pot over medium-high heat, stir together vinegar, sugar, mustard seeds, mustard, turmeric, pepper, fenugreek and cumin, and cook, stirring, until sugar has dissolved. Remove and set aside 2 cups (500 mL). Into same pot, stir reserved cucumber mixture; bring to a boil and immediately reduce to a simmer. Cook until cucumbers and onions are soft and have released their juices, at least 30 minutes. In bowl, whisk together cornstarch and reserved vinegar mixture; stir into pot. Increase heat to high and, stirring constantly, return to a boil and cook until thickened. Reduce heat and simmer for 3 minutes; transfer to sterilized Mason jars and seal, according to manufacturer's instructions.

Makes eight 500 mL Mason jars

BEST BREAKFAST SANDWICH
WITH MAPLE *and* APPLE SAUSAGE
WITH CHEDDAR AND ONION BISCUITS

This fun recipe is a respectful poke at the Tim Hortons' breakfast sandwich that so many of us have grabbed at a drive-through. Buttermilk biscuits are the base for these cheddar and onion biscuits. And making sausage patties is dead easy; it's basically the same as making a hamburger patty, so don't be put off. Give it a try, and I'll bet you'll never go through a drive-through for breakfast again! Well, then again, who am I kidding?

BREAKFAST SANDWICH INGREDIENTS

1 large tomato
Salt and pepper to taste
1 avocado
2 tbsp (30 mL) butter
6 eggs
Mayonnaise
Cheddar and Onion Biscuits (recipe follows), warmed and halved
Maple and Apple Sausage (recipe follows)
6 slices Cheddar (optional)

METHOD

Cut tomato into 6 thin slices; transfer to paper towel to drain and sprinkle with salt and pepper. Halve and pit avocado; with butter knife, cut cross-hatch into flesh, spacing cuts about ¼ inch (5 mm) apart. Scoop chunks of flesh into bowl.

In nonstick skillet, melt butter; fry eggs to preferred doneness (I recommend over easy, so the yolk is runny and delicious).

Spread mayonnaise over cut sides of each biscuit. On bottom of each, stack tomato slice, Maple and Apple Sausage, and avocado. If desired, add a slice of cheddar before replacing biscuit top.

Makes 6 breakfast sandwiches

CHEDDAR AND ONION BISCUITS INGREDIENTS

2 cups (500 mL) all-purpose flour
2 tsp (10 mL) baking powder
2 tsp (10 mL) granulated sugar
¼ tsp (1 mL) salt
¼ cup (60 mL) butter
3 green onions (green parts only), chopped
¾ cup (175 mL) grated aged Cheddar
3 eggs
2 cups (500 mL) buttermilk, plus extra for brushing

METHOD

In large bowl, whisk together flour, baking powder, sugar and salt. With 2 knives or pastry cutter, cut in butter until mixture is mealy. Stir in green onion tops and Cheddar; form well in centre.

In second bowl, beat eggs into buttermilk; pour into well in flour mixture. With fork, stir together by running fork along side of bowl down to centre, then out and up again; spin bowl as you work (this method prevents flour at bottom of bowl from remaining unmixed and incorporates all ingredients more quickly).

On lightly floured surface, knead only 2 to 3 times to form single ball (do not overwork); with palms, evenly pat dough to 1-inch (2.5 cm) thickness. With 4-inch (10 cm) biscuit cutter, cut out 6 rounds; transfer to parchment paper–lined baking sheet. (Gather and press remaining dough, then cut final biscuit; this one will be irregular, so enjoy it as the "cook's bonus.") Brush biscuit top with buttermilk; bake in 400°F (200°C) oven for 12 to 14 minutes.

Makes 6 biscuits

After you cut the first 6 rounds of biscuits from the dough, there will be a little scrap left over. This can be formed into a seventh biscuit, though it will not be as tender, simply because re-forming it will strengthen the gluten. However, we call these nibbly bits "the cook's share," so don't waste any of it. It still tastes great!

MAPLE AND APPLE SAUSAGE
INGREDIENTS

1 tbsp (15 mL) butter

½ small onion, minced

1 tsp (5 mL) summer savory

Pinch cayenne pepper

¼ cup (60 mL) apple juice or cider

1 egg, beaten

1 small apple, unpeeled and grated

1 lb (500 g) fresh pork sausage

½ cup (125 mL) fresh or dry bread crumbs

3 tbsp (45 mL) pure maple syrup

1 tbsp (15 mL) chopped fresh sage

¼ tsp (1 mL) salt

¼ tsp (1 mL) pepper

Vegetable oil

METHOD

In saucepan, melt butter; sauté onion, summer savory and cayenne pepper until onion is softened and translucent. Stir in apple juice and cook until only about 2 tbsp (30 mL) liquid remains. Scrape into bowl along with egg, apple, sausage, bread crumbs, maple syrup, sage, salt and pepper; with hands, thoroughly mix, then divide and form into six 4-ounce (125 g) patties. Wrap and refrigerate for about 1 hour to firm up.

In nonstick skillet, heat oil; fry patties for about 2 minutes per side. Reduce heat and keep warm until ready to use.

FINNAN HADDIE

The Scots who moved to Cape Breton introduced this chowder-like soup to Nova Scotia, and if you visit any pub in Scotland, you'll still find this dish on the menu. Marie Nightingale wrote *about finnan haddie in 1970, when* Out of Old Nova Scotia Kitchens *was first published. After several trips to Scotland and lots of "work-related" research, I created this version.*

INGREDIENTS

¼ cup (60 mL) butter

2 cloves garlic, minced

2 stalks celery, minced

1 onion, minced

2 cups (500 mL) thinly sliced leeks

Pinch each salt and pepper

4 cups (1 L) whole milk

3 cups (750 mL) grated potatoes

2 cups (500 mL) chicken stock

1 cup (250 mL) heavy cream (35% mf)

Pinch nutmeg

Sachet of fresh thyme, 8 peppercorns, 4 whole cloves,
   3 bay leaves and 1 star anise

1 lb (500 g) smoked haddock fillets

METHOD

In large heavy-bottomed pot or Dutch oven over medium heat, melt butter; sauté garlic, celery, onion, leeks, salt and pepper until vegetables are just beginning to soften but not colour. Stir in milk, potatoes, chicken stock, cream, nutmeg and sachet of herbs and spices; place haddock fillets on top and gently press into liquid until immersed. Reduce heat, cover and simmer until haddock flakes apart and potatoes dissolve and thicken chowder, about 1 hour.

With slotted spoon, transfer haddock to plate and let cool enough to handle; with fingers, flake apart and return to pot. Remove and discard sachet; cook until haddock is heated through.

Makes about 12 cups (3 L) or 8 large bowls

 A sachet is used in classical cooking to add aromatic flavours to soups, broths, or sauces. Fresh herbs are placed on a small piece of cheesecloth and tied into a bundle secured with butcher's twine. The sachet can be easily removed after simmering and discarded.

SEAFOOD CHOWDER

Chowder may be the most stereotypical dish on any restaurant menu in Nova Scotia, and that's because everyone who likes seafood loves chowder. Here, competitions are held for chowder glory and everyone thinks their mother makes the best. This is my shot at perfect chowder — free of pomp and ceremony, but full of the best seafood in the province. The innovation is the puréed soup base, to which the seafood is added. For most chowders, I serve tea biscuits or good warm bread, and garnish with some freshly ground black pepper.

INGREDIENTS

2 lb (1 kg) mussels

¼ cup (60 mL) butter

2 stalks celery, coarsely chopped

2 cloves garlic, halved

1 large onion, thinly sliced

½ fennel bulb (white parts only), thinly sliced

½ tsp (2 mL) salt

½ tsp (2 mL) pepper

2 cups (500 mL) white wine

6 cups (1.5 L) diced potatoes

3 bay leaves

3 cups (750 mL) whole milk

2 cups (500 mL) chicken stock

1 small 8 fl oz (250 mL) can baby clams, with juice

1 tsp (5 mL) thyme

1 tsp (5 mL) dillweed

1 ½ cups (375 mL) water

1 ½ cups (375 mL) heavy cream (35% mf)

2 lb (1 kg) haddock fillets, cut in 1-inch (2.5 cm) pieces

2 lb (1 kg) scallops, large ones halved

1 lb (500 g) frozen North Atlantic cold-water shrimp

8 oz (250 g) cooked lobster meat, coarsely chopped

2 tbsp (30 mL) chopped parsley or fresh tarragon (optional)

Freshly ground black pepper, for garnish

METHOD

Under cold running water, scrub and de-beard mussels, discarding any that are damaged or don't close when lightly tapped. Set aside.

In large saucepan over medium heat, melt butter; sauté celery, garlic, onion, fennel, salt and pepper until onion and fennel are translucent, about 5 minutes. Stir in ½ cup (125 mL) of the wine; cook, scraping up brown bits from bottom and sides of pan, until wine has evaporated. Stir in potatoes, bay leaves, milk, chicken stock, clams and juice, thyme and dillweed; reduce heat and simmer, stirring occasionally, until potatoes are softened and falling apart. Remove and discard bay leaves. Remove from heat and set aside.

Meanwhile, in large pot, bring remaining wine to a boil; add reserved mussels and let steam until opened, about 5 minutes. With tongs and reserving cooking liquid, transfer mussels to plate and let cool enough to handle. Discarding any unopened mussels, pick meat from shells and transfer to bowl. Set aside. Carefully pour cooking liquid into large glass measure, leaving any sand or grit in bottom of pot; transfer to second bowl and add reserved mussels. Cover and refrigerate until ready to use.

In batches in food processor, purée reserved celery mixture until blended and smooth, leaving lid vented but covering with tea towel, and starting at very low speed for each batch, then increasing speed as it batch purées. Transfer into clean pot; stir in heavy cream and bring to a simmer. Stir in haddock, scallops, shrimp, lobster and reserved cooking liquid; simmer until haddock flakes easily with fork, about 20 minutes. Garnish with parsley and freshly ground black pepper.

Makes 6 to 8 entrée servings

SNOW CRAB CAKES
with GUACAMOLE

{ *Our snow crabs in Cape Breton are some of the best in the world and available year-round. I've been getting mine from a small co-operative in Neil's Harbour for a few years now, and I've never tasted better crab anywhere in the world. Crab cakes are a favourite appetizer and party food for people here. My*

version is paired with creamy avocado, not a Nova Scotian ingredient by far, but one that represents the Caribbean immigrants who landed and worked in Cape Breton for many years and who brought a new and interesting flavour base to some familiar dishes. }

SNOW CRAB CAKES
INGREDIENTS

1 lb (500 g) snow crab meat

2 tbsp (30 mL) butter

2 shallots, minced

1 clove garlic, minced

1 stalk celery, minced

Pinch each salt and pepper

¼ cup (60 mL) white wine

1 egg

½ cup (125 mL) mayonnaise

1 tbsp (15 mL) Dijon mustard

½ tsp (2 mL) Worcestershire sauce

2 to 3 dashes hot sauce

Zest and juice of 1 lemon

3 green onions, finely chopped

1 ½ cups (375 mL) fresh or panko bread crumbs

3 eggs, beaten

½ cup (125 mL) all-purpose flour

Salt and pepper to taste

4 cups (1 L) vegetable oil

Guacamole (recipe follows)

Sprigs of cilantro (optional)

Chipotle Mayo (see page 151)

METHOD

In colander, squeeze crabmeat to remove excess moisture. In saucepan over medium heat, melt butter; sauté shallots, garlic, celery, salt and pepper until vegetables are softened and translucent. Stir in wine and cook, scraping any brown bits from bottom and sides of pan, until wine has evaporated and pan is dry. Remove from heat; set aside and let cool.

In large bowl, whisk together egg, mayonnaise, mustard, Worcestershire sauce, hot sauce and lemon zest and juice. Stir shallot mixture. Fold in crab meat, green onions and ¾ cup (175 mL) of the bread crumbs until thoroughly mixed.

With hands, evenly divide crab-meat mixture and form into 8 or 16 patties. Cover and refrigerate for at least 1 hour to firm up before starting the breading process.

Into shallow dish, pour eggs. In second shallow dish, whisk together flour, salt and pepper. Into third shallow dish, pour remaining panko bread crumbs. One at a time, dip patties into flour mixture, then the egg mixture to coat all over, and then in bread crumbs.

In large, steep-sided pot, heat oil until thermometer registers 350°F (180°C); with slotted spoon, transfer patties to oil and cook until crisp, golden and heated through, 2 to 4 minutes. Garnish each with Guacamole and, if desired, sprig of cilantro.

As an additional accompaniment for this dish, serve it with my Chipotle Mayo recipe (page 151) as a dipping sauce. The extra spiciness works well to balance the buttery mouth feel of the guacamole.

Makes 8 appetizers or 18 hors d'oeuvres

> *For me, these should be moist inside, as I dislike dry, mealy crab cakes. Therefore, the filling is quite soft to handle. When they are removed from the fridge they will have set a bit, but they still may lose some of their shape as you transfer them from flour, to eggwash, to breadcrumbs. But the crab cakes can be reshaped easily once the breadcrumbs are applied, so don't panic if they lose their shape as you handle them.*

GUACAMOLE
INGREDIENTS

2 ripe avocados

2 green onions (green parts only), sliced

1 clove garlic, minced

2 tbsp (30 mL) minced red onion

2 tbsp (30 mL) chopped fresh cilantro

1 tbsp (15 mL) extra-virgin olive oil

Juice of 1 lime

Dash Tabasco sauce

Pinch salt

METHOD

Halve and pit avocados; with butter knife, cut cross-hatch into flesh, spacing cuts about ¼ inch (5 mm) apart. Scoop chunks of flesh into bowl; fold in green onion tops, garlic, onion, cilantro, oil, lime juice, Tabasco sauce and salt just until mixed but slightly chunky.

Makes 1 ½ cups (375 mL)

SMOKED SALMON PIZZA

Nova Scotia produces plenty of smoked salmon, and pizza will always will be a beloved dish. This makes them perfect partners! In just a few steps, this recipe offers complex flavours that still let the salmon shine. I recommend using a pizza stone for this or any thin-crust pizza, and a high heat

to crisp the crust. I created this dish in my home kitchen with my faithful recipe tester Jacqueline with me, and we both agreed that a few chives on top as garnish was all this needed, as the flavours within were bold and tangy.

INGREDIENTS

1 cup (250 mL) full-fat sour cream

1/2 cup (125 mL) creamy goat cheese

1 tbsp (15 mL) capers

1 tbsp (15 mL) chopped dillweed

Zest and juice of 1/2 lemon

Pepper to taste

Pizza Dough (recipe follows)

1/4 cup (60 mL) extra-virgin olive oil, plus extra for drizzle

3/4 cup (175 mL) thinly sliced red onions

1 tsp (5 mL) coarse sea salt

1/4 English cucumber, finely sliced

1 lb (500 g) smoked salmon, thinly sliced

2 tbsp (30 mL) minced fresh chives

Brushing the dough with oil is key to this recipe as it prevents the dough in the middle from rising too much as it bakes. This is also the reason the oil is not brushed on the outer crust, as you want this to rise to form a light, crispy edge, one of the characteristics of a great thin-crust pizza.

METHOD

In food processor, pulse together sour cream, goat cheese, capers, dillweed, lemon zest and juice until smooth and blended. Transfer to bowl, cover and refrigerate until ready to use.

Place pizza stone in 500°F (260°C) oven to heat. With palm, flatten dough; with fingertips, gently massage, pulling it into 12-inch (30 cm) circle of even thickness; transfer to lightly floured rimless baking sheet, reshaping circle, if necessary. Leaving 3/4-inch (2 cm) border around edge of crust, brush dough with oil and evenly sprinkle with onions and salt. With quick jolt, slide dough from baking sheet onto hot pizza stone; bake until crisp, golden and cooked through, 7 to 10 minutes. Repeat the process for a second pizza if desired.

Transfer crust to baking sheet or cutting board. Evenly spread crust with half of reserved sour cream mixture; top with layer of half the cucumber. Arrange half the smoked salmon in single layer overtop, completely covering crust; with sharp chef's knife, cut pizza into 6 or 8 slices and sprinkle with about 1 tbsp (15 mL) of the minced chives. Drizzle with oil. Repeat process for second pizza if desired.

Makes two 12-inch (30 cm) pizzas

PIZZA DOUGH
INGREDIENTS

1 ¾ cups (425 mL) lukewarm water

1 tbsp (15 mL) liquid honey

1 package active dry yeast

4 cups (1 L) type 00 fine Italian flour, plus extra for dusting

2 tsp (10 mL) sea salt

2 tbsp (30 mL) extra-virgin olive oil

METHOD

In glass measure, gently stir together water, honey and yeast until honey and yeast are dissolved.

In large bowl, whisk together flour and salt; form well in centre. Into well, pour water mixture and oil; with fork, mix, scraping sides of bowl just until loose dough comes together. On lightly floured surface, knead, adding dusting of flour if dough is too sticky, until dough is smooth and elastic, about 10 minutes. With hands, form into ball, dust with flour and transfer to bowl; cover with damp tea towel and let rise in warm, draft-free spot until doubled in size, 1 to 1 ½ hours. Halve dough and form each half into ball. Use immediately or wrap with plastic wrap and refrigerate (or freeze) until ready to use.

Makes two 12-inch (30 cm) pizza crusts

THE HALIFAX
DONAIR

Quintessential Halifax street food, the donair has connections to many Old World dishes called doner kebabs. Roasted lamb, pork and beef on a skewer garnished with pickles and a tangy or spicy sauce, then wrapped in a flatbread — this classic has been served for hundreds of years by many world cultures. It's also the only Nova Scotian food that signals a specific city (Halifax), similar to other iconic foods such as the Philly cheese-steak sandwich (Philadelphia), smoked meat sandwiches and poutine (Montreal), beaver tails (Ottawa) or clam chowder (Boston). The sauce makes the donair, and that's why the Halifax version is cherished. You either love 'em or hate 'em. I adore 'em. I've created this recipe to mimic the spit-roasting and carving of the meat you find in a donair shop. It's easy to make and tastes exactly like a donair you'd wolf down at 2 a.m. to finish a night on the town. Grab yourself a big handful of napkins and tuck in!

INGREDIENTS

3 lb (1.5 kg) lean ground beef

1 cup (250 mL) fine bread crumbs

¼ cup (60 mL) water

2 tbsp (30 mL) canola oil, plus extra for greasing and frying

1 tbsp (15 mL) garlic powder

1 tbsp (15 mL) onion powder

1 tbsp (15 mL) pepper

1 tbsp (15 mL) oregano

2 tsp (10 mL) beef bouillon powder

1 tsp (5 mL) cayenne pepper

1 tsp (5 mL) salt

6 pita rounds (7-in/18 cm diameter)

2 cups (500 mL) Classic Donair Sauce (recipe follows)

2 tomatoes, diced

1 small onion, diced

METHOD

In stand mixer fitted with dough hook, combine beef, bread crumbs, water, oil, garlic powder, onion powder, pepper, oregano, bouillon powder, cayenne pepper and salt. On low speed, process until liquid has incorporated, then slowly increase speed to knead donair mixture until pasty and sticking to sides, at least 10 minutes.

Layer two 24-inch/60 cm lengths of foil on work surface; lightly grease top with food-release spray or canola oil. With hands, evenly divide donair mixture into 4 piles, side by side, lengthwise along centre of foil; shape into log about 14 -to 16-inches (35 to 40 cm) long. Tightly roll foil around log, compressing donair mixture; tightly twist foil at each end to seal. Transfer to rimmed baking sheet; bake in 325°F (160°C) oven until internal-read thermometer in centre of log registers 160°F (71°C), about 90 minutes. Immediately transfer to deep baking dish, surround with ice and refrigerate for at least 4 hours, preferably overnight.

Preheat oven to broil; slide top rack into top slot. Holding roll upright on cutting board, remove foil from donair; with very sharp knife, slice long ribbons of meat down cylinder and transfer in loose pile to rimmed baking sheet. Broil for 1 minute; remove from oven and, with tongs, toss. Return to oven and broil for 1 minute. In same manner, toss and broil until donair mixture is browned and heated through, about 4 times.

Fill large bowl with cold water; set aside. In large nonstick skillet over medium heat, warm small amount of canola oil; one at a time, quickly dip pitas into water, immediately transfer to pan and cook until edges are beginning to brown, about 30 seconds per side.

Place each warm pita on plate (or foil square for takeout-style); top with heaping 1 tbsp (15 mL) Classic Donair Sauce and sprinkle with tomatoes and onion. Evenly divide donair meat among pitas; top with 2 to 3 tbsp (30 to 45 mL) Classic Donair Sauce. If serving takeout-style, roll 2 opposite sides of pita over filling, then roll donair in foil, tucking in foil at one end but leaving other (top end) open.

Makes 6 donairs

Although donair meat can be made by hand in a mixing bowl, it is much better to use a stand-up electric mixer and choose the dough-hook attachment to get the meat properly mixed. As the meat mixes, the proteins and fats emulsify and help to create the firm, chewy texture of the donair, a signature component of the dish. Without working the meat, the resulting texture will be more crumbly, similar to meatloaf or hamburger. Finally, carving the donair lengthwise once it has cooled and firmed up closely resembles how the meat is traditionally shaved off the spit roaster in a takeout donair shop.

CLASSIC DONAIR SAUCE
INGREDIENTS
1 can (12 oz/370 mL) full-fat evaporated milk
³/₄ cup (175 mL) granulated sugar
1 tsp (5 mL) garlic powder
¹/₃ cup (75 mL) white vinegar

METHOD
In bowl, stir together milk and sugar; evenly sprinkle with garlic powder and gently whisk until sugar has dissolved. Whisk in vinegar, scraping sides, until thickened. Transfer to airtight container and refrigerate for at least 2 hours, up to 12 hours, to thicken as it cools.

Makes 1 ¹/₂ cups (375 mL)

CHICKEN DINNER
POUTINE

{ *Roast chicken dinner with bread stuffing infused with summer savory is a long-time Nova Scotia favourite, while poutine has become a new staple on restaurant menus in just a few* *decades. This dish captures all the goodness of a home-cooked meal from a country kitchen and includes our chef de cuisine Andrew (a.k.a. Cookie) Farrell's family stuffing recipe.* }

INGREDIENTS

1 tbsp (15 mL) butter
½ cup (125 mL) frozen sweet peas
About 1 tsp (5 mL) water
Chip Wagon French Fries (page 50)
Pulled Chicken and Poutine Gravy (recipe follows)
Cookie's Mom's Stuffing (recipe follows)
2 cups (500 mL) salted cheese curds, at room temperature
1 tbsp (15 mL) chopped parsley or fresh sage

METHOD

In small saucepan, melt butter; sauté peas with water until tender and heated through. If necessary, reheat Chip Wagon French Fries, Pulled Chicken and Poutine Gravy, and Cookie's Mom's Stuffing.

Half-fill 4 deep warmed bowls with Chip Wagon French Fries; generously scatter with cheese curds. Top with Cookie's Mom's Stuffing, Pulled Chicken, peas and Poutine Gravy. Garnish with parsley.

PULLED CHICKEN AND POUTINE GRAVY
INGREDIENTS

4 skin-on chicken leg-and-thigh quarters
Salt and pepper to taste
4 cloves garlic, coarsely chopped
1 onion, coarsely chopped
1 carrot, diced
1 stalk celery, diced
2 tbsp (30 mL) olive oil
3 cups (750 mL) chicken stock
1 tsp (5 mL) summer savory

METHOD

On rimmed baking sheet, arrange chicken and sprinkle with salt and pepper. In bowl, toss together garlic, onion, carrot and celery; evenly arrange over second rimmed baking sheet; drizzle with oil and lightly toss with fingers. Transfer both sheets to oven; bake in 400°F (200°C) oven until chicken skin is golden brown, about 40 minutes.

Remove from oven; transfer chicken and vegetable mixture to same large pot. Add chicken stock and summer savory. One at a time, place roasting pans on high heat; add ladle of chicken stock. Cook, scraping up brown bits from bottom and sides of pans with wooden spoon; transfer scraping mixture to large pot. Cover and simmer chicken mixture until chicken is tender and falling off bones, 30 to 45 minutes. Remove chicken from the pot using a slotted spoon. When cool enough to touch, pull the meat from the bones and skin; place the meat in a bowl and keep warm; discard the bones, skin, and cartilage that remains.

Bring vegetable mixture in cooking liquid to a boil; with immersion blender, purée gravy until blended and smooth. If desired, add salt and pepper.

Makes 4 entrées or 8 snacks

This recipe can be made easier by cooking the chicken and making the gravy in advance. Pulled chicken meat reheats easily either in the microwave or in a saucepan with a little of the gravy thrown in for moisture. The dressing can be done the same way, although reheating that in the oven will give some crispy edges that taste great.

COOKIE'S MOM'S STUFFING
INGREDIENTS

1 loaf whole wheat bread, torn in small pieces
1 cup (250 mL) butter
2 carrots, grated
1 stalk celery, finely chopped
1 onion, finely chopped
½ tsp (2 mL) salt
1 tsp (5 mL) pepper
1 tbsp (15 mL) summer savory
4 green onions, chopped
1 cup (250 mL) chicken stock

METHOD

On 2 rimmed baking sheets, evenly spread bread; bake in 350°F (180°C) oven until browned and slightly dry, tossing once or twice; about 5 to 7 minutes.

Meanwhile, in saucepan over medium-high heat, melt butter; sweat carrots, celery, onion, salt and pepper until onion and celery are softened and translucent, 5 to 7 minutes.

In bowl, toss bread and carrot mixture along with summer savoury and green onions until bread has absorbed butter; stir in chicken stock. Transfer to casserole or lasagne dish; bake in 350°F (180°C) oven until top is browned, about 10 minutes. Remove from heat; cover and refrigerate until ready to use.

Makes 8 cups (2 L)

THAI GREEN CHICKEN CURRY

When my friend and colleague Marie Nightingale wrote Out of Old Nova Scotia Kitchens in 1970, I am quite sure she never would have considered including a Thai green curry recipe as a featured entrée. But the one thing that always impressed me about Marie — my Nova Scotia culinary idol — was her love of all the wonderful new dishes and flavours introduced to the province. Honestly, can you even imagine our cities and towns without sushi restaurants? I certainly can't. I don't know if Marie ever made any curry, but I do know that she was immensely proud of every hardworking young chef and cook who enriched Nova Scotia's culinary landscape. In Halifax, Thai restaurants are incredibly popular — the food is full of bright, balanced flavours and endless variety. Like Marie, I'm grateful to live in a city that embraces so many different types of cuisine.

INGREDIENTS

Two 8 fl oz cans (500 mL) coconut milk

Green Curry Paste (recipe follows)

3 boneless skinless chicken breasts (about 8 oz/250 g each), thinly sliced

2 carrots, thinly sliced on diagonal

1 red onion, coarsely chopped

1 sweet red pepper, coarsely chopped

1 small 6 fl oz can (200 mL) bamboo shoots

Big handful fresh snow peas

1 cup (250 mL) sliced shiitake mushrooms

4 green onions, cut in 1-inch (2.5 cm) lengths

METHOD

In large saucepan or wok, bring coconut milk to a boil; whisk in Green Curry Paste until blended and smooth. Return to a boil; stir in chicken, carrots, onion, red pepper, bamboo shoots, snow peas, mushrooms and green onions and simmer just until chicken is firm and cooked through, 5 to 7 minutes.

Makes 4 servings

GREEN CURRY PASTE
INGREDIENTS

1 stalk lemongrass, tough outer leaves removed

8 green chili peppers, halved and seeded

5 cloves garlic

2 shallots, coarsely chopped

1 bunch cilantro, thoroughly washed and coarsely chopped

1 piece gingerroot (about 2-in/5 cm long), coarsely chopped

Zest and juice of 1 lime

2 tbsp (30 mL) fish sauce

2 tbsp (30 mL) soy sauce

2 tbsp (30 mL) liquid honey

2 tsp (10 mL) sesame oil

2 tsp (10 mL) cumin seeds

2 tsp (10 mL) coriander seeds

½ tsp (2 mL) salt

METHOD

Finely chop lemongrass; transfer to large glass measure. Toss in chili peppers, garlic, shallots, cilantro, gingerroot, lime zest and juice, fish sauce, soy sauce, honey, oil, cumin seeds, coriander seeds and salt to thoroughly mix. Transfer to food processor; process on high, scraping down sides once or twice, until blended and smooth. If not using immediately, transfer to airtight container and refrigerate for up to 7 days.

Makes 1 ¼ cups (310 mL)

SMOKEHOUSE SLIDERS

WITH SMOKED GOUDA CHEESE SLICES; SCOTCH BARBECUE SAUCE; CARAMELIZED ONION, BACON AND BALSAMIC JAM; CHIPOTLE MAYO AND CRISPY FRIED SHALLOTS

The burger may be as all-American as apple pie, but burger mania is also big in Nova Scotia. Chef Andrew Farrell and I created a burger that stands up to any burger anywhere. Andrew created this version for our Halifax Burger Week festival and it's a real crowd-pleaser. The little garnishes are worth the effort to make and the barbecue sauce, chipotle mayo and bacon jam will keep refrigerated for a week or so, if you make a larger batch. We make our own cheese because we love the creamy, wonderful richness of an American-style cheese, but you can certainly replace that with regular smoked Gouda, Cheddar or any favourite cheese.

SMOKEHOUSE SLIDERS
INGREDIENTS

2 lb (1 kg) boneless short rib roast, cut in 1 ½-inch (2.5 cm) cubes

2 lb (1 kg) chuck roast, cut in 1 ½-inch (2.5 cm) cubes

2 lb (1 kg) brisket roast, cut in 1 ½-inch (2.5 cm) cubes

Salt and pepper to taste

12 large slider buns

12 Smoked Gouda Cheese Slices (recipe follows)

Chipotle Mayo (recipe follows)

Crispy Fried Shallots (recipe follows)

1 cup (125 mL) Scotch Barbecue Sauce (recipe follows)

½ cup (125 mL) Caramelized Onion, Bacon and Balsamic Jam
   (recipe follows)

2 cups (500 mL) arugula leaves

METHOD

In bowl, toss together short rib roast cubes, chuck roast cubes and brisket roast cubes until thoroughly mixed; with meat grinder or stand mixer fitted with a standard meat grinding attachment, feed through machine to grind, then pass through machine grinder again (for coarse, "steak-like" mouth feel, you can grind only once, but I recommend grinding twice). With hands, form into twenty-four 4-ounce (125 g) 3 ½-inch (9 cm) patties; layer between plastic wrap and refrigerate until very cold.

Preheat one end of barbecue to high and the other to low (so you can start cooking on high then move patties over lower heat if burning), grill to desired doneness (since beef is fresh-ground, medium doneness is safe), turning once. Remove from heat and sprinkle with salt and pepper; let stand for 5 minutes. Meanwhile, toast buns on grill or warm in oven. Remove from heat.

Open buns on work surface, cut side up; tear each Gouda Cheese Slice in half and place half on each top and bottom of buns. Spread bottoms of buns with Chipotle Mayo and heaping 1 tsp (5 mL) Crispy Fried Shallots. Top each with patty and spread with Caramelized Onion, Bacon and Balsamic Jam. Place 2 or 3 arugula leaves over each patty; replace bun tops.

Makes 12 sliders (6 entrée servings or 12 appetizers)

My recipe uses 2 pounds (1 kg) ground beef, which yields twenty-four 4-ounce (125 g) patties. You can use 12 right away, then wrap and freeze 12 to use later — or make more and form some full-size burger patties, as well. It's totally up to you, so make as much as you like — it's the ratio that counts!

SMOKED GOUDA CHEESE SLICES
INGREDIENTS

3 tbsp (45 mL) gelatin powder

1 1/2 tbsp (22 mL) water

1 cup (250 mL) whole milk

2 lb (1 kg) shredded smoked Gouda cheese, at room temperature

3 tbsp (45 mL) whole milk powder

1 tbsp (15 mL) salt

1/4 tsp (1 mL) cream of tartar

METHOD

In small glass measure, sprinkle gelatin into water; let stand for about 5 minutes. In saucepan, bring milk almost to a boil; immediately stir in gelatin mixture until dissolved. Remove from heat.

In food processor, place Gouda, milk powder, salt and cream of tartar; pour gelatin mixture overtop. Pulse, scraping down sides once or twice, until smooth and blended, about 3 minutes. With spatula, scrape into plastic wrap-lined loaf pan or terrine; cover with plastic wrap and refrigerate for at least 12 hours.

Turn out of mould; slice with very sharp knife or cheese plane.

Makes 2 lb (1 kg) block of cheese

SCOTCH BARBECUE SAUCE
INGREDIENTS

2 tbsp (30 mL) canola oil

3 cloves garlic, coarsely chopped

1 onion, coarsely chopped

1 tsp (5 mL) pepper

1/2 tsp (2 mL) sea salt

1 cup (250 mL) single malt Scotch whisky

1 can (125 mL) tomato paste

2 cups (500 mL) ketchup

1 cup (250 mL) molasses

3/4 cup (175 mL) red wine vinegar

3/4 cup (175 mL) packed brown sugar

1/4 cup (60 mL) Worcestershire sauce

2 tbsp (30 mL) Dijon mustard

1 tbsp (15 mL) liquid smoke

2 tsp (10 mL) Tabasco sauce

METHOD

In saucepan, warm oil; sauté garlic, onion, pepper and salt until onion is translucent and beginning to brown, about 3 minutes. Carefully add whisky and ignite (flambé) the alcohol; when alcohol has completely evaporated, stir in tomato paste, ketchup, molasses, vinegar, brown sugar, Worcestershire sauce, mustard, liquid smoke and Tabasco sauce. Reduce heat and gently simmer until thickened, about 30 minutes. With immersion blender, purée until blended and smooth; transfer to airtight container. Let cool; refrigerate until ready to use.

If you're using a gas stove, move saucepan away from open flame when pouring in the whisky, then return the pan back to the burner and carefully tilt it just until the whisky ignites. When lighting a flambé on an electric range, use a long wooden match or, even better, a barbecue lighter.

Makes 3 1/2 cups (875 mL)

CARAMELIZED ONION, BACON AND BALSAMIC JAM
INGREDIENTS

1 lb (500 g) smoked bacon, cut in ½-inch (5 cm) lengths
½ cup (125 mL) water
2 lb (1 kg) white or red onions, sliced
¼ tsp (1 mL) salt
½ tsp (2 mL) pepper
½ cup (125 mL) balsamic vinegar
¼ cup (60 mL) liquid honey
2 tbsp (30 mL) packed brown sugar

METHOD

In large saucepan over medium heat, combine bacon and water; cook until water has evaporated and bacon is crisp and browned, about 10 minutes. Reserving fat in pan, with slotted spoon, transfer bacon to paper towel to drain.

To pan, add onions, salt and pepper; increase heat to high and cook for about 5 minutes. Reduce heat to medium-low; cook until onions are beginning to caramelize, 20 to 30 minutes. Stir in vinegar, honey and brown sugar and cook, stirring occasionally, until liquid has evaporated and onions are glazed, sticky and dark. Stir in bacon and cook just until warmed through.

Makes 2 ½ cups (625 mL)

CHIPOTLE MAYO
INGREDIENTS

1 cup (250 mL) mayonnaise
1 tbsp (15 mL) chipotle pepper purée, jarred or tinned
1 tsp (5 mL) lemon juice
Pinch each salt and pepper

METHOD

In small bowl, stir together mayonnaise, chipotle pepper purée, lemon juice, salt and pepper until blended and smooth. Cover and refrigerate until ready to use.

Makes 1 cup (250 mL)

CRISPY FRIED SHALLOTS
INGREDIENTS

½ cup (125 mL) cornstarch
6 shallots
2 cups (500 mL) canola, vegetable or peanut oil
Salt (optional)

METHOD

Place cornstarch in shallow dish. Finely slice shallots; gently separate slices into rounds. Dredge shallots in cornstarch to coat all over.

In deep, steep-sided saucepan, heat oil until thermometer registers 350°F (180°C); add shallots and cook until crisp and golden. With slotted spoon, transfer to paper towel to drain; sprinkle with salt, if desired. Let cool; transfer to airtight container and store at room temperature until ready to use.

Makes 1 cup (250 mL)

CHOCOLATE RUM CAKE
with CHOCOLATE GANACHE
AND TOASTED-COCONUT ICE CREAM

This dessert is a nod to our rum-running traditions in Nova Scotia and a testament to how chocolate is forever loved by all, year-round. The flavours of chocolate, rum, coffee and coconut are magical together, and although they may not be natively grown in our province, for me, they are essentials in cooking. There are many examples of how imported ingredients and cultural influences become our own. Can you imagine a valley apple pie without cinnamon? A winter's afternoon without tea? Fish and chips without a squeeze of lemon? I love the way this dessert symbolizes our unique heritage in the province and how our cooking has evolved along with our hearts and minds. This cake is very dense, almost like a French-style ganache torte, so a little goes a long way.

CHOCOLATE RUM CAKE
INGREDIENTS

6 oz (175 g) dark chocolate (at least 70% cacao), finely chopped

2 tbsp (30 mL) instant coffee

2 cups (500 mL) all-purpose flour, plus extra for dusting pan

1 tsp (5 mL) baking powder

1 cup (250 mL) granulated sugar, plus 2 tbsp (30 mL) for syrup

1 cup (250 mL) packed brown sugar

½ lb (250 g) salted butter, plus extra for greasing pan

1 tsp (5 mL) vanilla extract or rum

4 eggs

1½ cups (375 mL) fresh-brewed coffee

½ cup (125 mL) dark rum, plus ¼ cup (60 mL) for syrup

2 tbsp (30 mL) water

Warm Chocolate Ganache (recipe follows)

Toasted Coconut Ice Cream (recipe follows)

METHOD

Place chocolate in heatproof bowl and set over saucepan of simmering water; gently stir until melted and smooth. Remove from heat; let cool slightly.

In spice grinder or with mortar and pestle, finely crush instant-coffee granules. In large bowl, whisk together flour, baking powder and instant-coffee granules. Set aside. Beat together sugar, brown sugar, butter and vanilla until light and smooth. One at a time, beat in eggs, beating to incorporate each addition, until blended and smooth. Beat in melted chocolate until blended and smooth.

In glass measure, combine brewed coffee and ½ cup (125 mL) dark rum. Alternately beat coffee mixture and flour mixture into butter mixture, scraping down sides, until batter is blended and smooth.

With flour, dust greased 9-inch (23 cm) Bundt pan, shaking out excess. Scrape batter into pan; bake in centre of 325°F (160°C) oven until cake tester inserted in centre comes out clean, about 1 hour. Remove from heat; let cool in pan on rack for 30 minutes. Unmould onto serving platter.

In small saucepan over medium heat, stir together 2 tbsp (30 mL) granulated sugar and water until sugar has dissolved. Stir in ¼ cup (60 mL) rum. Brush syrup all over top of cake until completely absorbed. Serve with Warm Chocolate Ganache and Toasted Coconut Ice Cream.

Makes 14 to 16 servings

CHOCOLATE GANACHE
INGREDIENTS

8 oz (250 g) finely chopped semisweet chocolate
1 cup (250 mL) heavy cream (35% mf)
1 tsp (5 mL) vanilla extract

METHOD

Place chocolate in heatproof bowl. In saucepan, bring cream just to
a boil; immediately remove from heat and whisk into chocolate along
with vanilla until blended and smooth. If not serving immediately,
transfer to airtight container and refrigerate until ready to use. Rewarm
sauce, stirring, before serving.

Makes 2 cups (500 mL)

TOASTED-COCONUT ICE CREAM
INGREDIENTS

1 cup (250 mL) shredded unsweetened coconut
2 cups (500 mL) milk
2 cups (500 mL) coconut milk
1 cup (250 mL) heavy cream (35% mf)
12 egg yolks
1 cup (250 mL) granulated sugar
1 tsp (5 mL) vanilla extract
Pinch salt

METHOD

Evenly spread coconut on rimmed baking sheet; bake in 350°F (180°C)
oven, stirring once or twice, until fragrant and slightly browned.

In saucepan over medium-high heat, stir together milk, coconut milk
and cream just until hot (do not boil); stir in coconut. Remove from heat;
let stand for 1 hour.

In heatproof bowl, beat together egg yolks, sugar, vanilla and salt
until light and creamy. Return milk mixture to stove over medium heat;
bring just to a simmer. Slowly whisk into egg yolk mixture; return to
pan over very low heat and cook, stirring constantly, until thickened
enough to coat back of spoon. Through fine-mesh sieve, strain into
bowl; cover and refrigerate over an ice bath, until chilled. Churn
the custard base in an ice cream machine as per manufacturer's
instructions.

Makes 8 cups (2 L) ice cream

CARROT PUDDING
with BROWN-SUGAR BRANDY SAUCE

I am very proud to have this recipe in this book. Donated by Ernie and Marilyn Hovell, my parents' neighbours in the Annapolis Valley, it is a cherished recipe from his grandmother and is served faithfully every Christmas in his family. It echoes a plum pudding, aromatic with seasonal spices and buttery in flavour. This is a recipe that is long forgotten in Nova Scotia, possibly first discovered and *published by Marie Nightingale in* Out of Old Nova Scotia Kitchens. *But this recipe is so unique it was handed to me on a photocopied, handwritten piece of paper in Ernie's grandmother's writing, from back in 1952. I am suggesting here that you use a brandy sauce derived from a standard brown-sugar sauce common in rural Nova Scotia. It gives that little extra bit of "Christmas" into each bite.*

CARROT PUDDING
INGREDIENTS

1 ½ cups (375 mL) bread crumbs
1 ½ cups (375 mL) packed brown sugar
¾ cup (175 mL) all-purpose flour
1 tsp (5 mL) cinnamon
¾ tsp (4 mL) baking soda
½ tsp (2 mL) nutmeg
½ tsp (2 mL) ground cloves
1 egg
2 cups (500 mL) raisins
1 cup (250 mL) grated carrots
1 cup (250 mL) grated apples
1 cup (250 mL) grated potatoes
1 cup (250 mL) shredded beef suet
⅓ cup (75 mL) mixed candied peel
Brown-Sugar Brandy Sauce (recipe follows)

METHOD

In bowl, stir together bread crumbs, brown sugar, flour, cinnamon, baking soda, nutmeg and cloves.

In large bowl, with fork, slightly beat egg; stir in raisins, carrots, apples, potatoes, suet and candied peel until thoroughly mixed. Stir in bread-crumb mixture to form thick wet batter. Scrape into greased baking dish; cover with plastic wrap.

Place steaming rack in large pot filled with enough water to come just below rack; set baking dish on rack, cover and steam over medium-high heat, topping up water if necessary, until cooked through, about 3 hours. Remove from heat. If not serving immediately, rewarm before serving. Serve with Brown Sugar Brandy Sauce.

Makes 8 to 10 servings

BROWN-SUGAR BRANDY SAUCE

½ cup (125 mL) salted butter, melted
½ cup (125 mL) packed brown sugar
2 tbsp (30 mL) brandy
½ cup (125 mL) heavy cream (35% mf)

METHOD

In saucepan over medium-high heat, stir together butter and brown sugar and cook, stirring, until sugar has dissolved. Stir in brandy, then cream, and bring to a boil; immediately remove from heat. Set aside and keep warm until ready to serve.

Makes 1 ½ cups (375 mL)

ACKNOWLEDGEMENTS

For me, writing a cookbook involves a lot of time staring either at a wall or a laptop screen thinking of recipes. But more than that, it involves the assistance and support of many people. I have wonderful staff in my businesses, as well as a lot of food-loving friends, and they all are invaluable in a project like this. I continue to learn from other cooks, and many of those people are cooking in my kitchens as I write these words. Their creativity and influence is crucial to what I do, and many of these recipes are the result of those collaborations. My business partners, chef de cuisines, sous chefs, chef de parties, apprentices and wonderful front-of-house staff have all contributed to this collection in many ways. Most importantly they have kept the businesses running and my restaurant guests happy and well fed, as they so often do when I become distracted by projects like this. I love and respect them all and absolutely could not have published this book without relying on them every day. A special shout out to Carissa Frenette, who was my assistant on all the photo shoots, prepping and keeping me organized for days on end, and all on her own time. Another to Lindsay Ruck and Jonathan James, who both helped test several recipes for me when it was crunch time.

In a few cases I have included here a recipe taken nearly word-for-word from old family archives, with credit given to the contributors. These are dishes I am particularly proud of, as I hope putting them into print will ensure that they are around for a very long time, to be enjoyed by more people than could have otherwise occurred. The people in this province who cook at home and keep traditional regional recipes alive deserve respect and praise, because I truly believe that our food heritage creates an identity and sense of place for Nova Scotia, as it does for every corner of the world.

The job of a cook to produce great tasting food is made infinitely easier when you are surrounded by a wealth of seasonal ingredients and artisan food products. The farmers, fishermen, cheese makers, wine makers, brew masters, butchers and specialty product geniuses in this province have helped make me look good for years thanks to their dedication to produce the best of everything. Thank you for doing all the hard work for cooks everywhere.

Thank you to the many guests that walk through the doors of my restaurants every day. A cook is nothing without a willing audience, and your patronage has kept me trying to improve my cooking and to be a better host. Thank you for coming back, for forgiving our mistakes and for supporting locally owned and operated restaurants. By doing so you help keep our food community on all sides of the farm and table growing and prospering.

Thank you to the team at Formac, especially Meghan Collins and Meredith Bangay for the design work, and to Jennifer Partridge for the great photography. As they say, "you eat with your eyes first," and the same rules apply with cookbooks. Thank you for your creativity and for designing a beautiful book.

I could never do any of this without the support of my family. It is around our tables at celebratory gatherings and it is in my mother's kitchen as a child that I first fell in love with good food made with love.

And last but not least, thank you to Jacqueline: my fiancée, bestie and chief recipe taster! I will forever remember fondly the many sessions we had together testing these dishes in our little kitchen in Dartmouth, grilling on the back deck, or walking through markets together dreaming up something new for dinner. I am raising a glass of Nova 7 to you and to many, many more meals together in our happy Nova Scotia home.

INDEX